MUNICH

GREAT CENTRES OF ART

MUNICH

A. S. BARNES AND COMPANY
SOUTH BRUNSWICK AND NEW YORK

Translated from the German by Sylvia Furness and revised by Professor D. Talbot Rice

First American Edition 1969
Published by A. S. Barnes and Co., Inc. Cranbury, N. J. 08512
New York 16, N. Y.
Copyright 1967 by Edition Leipzig and © 1967 by Süddeutscher Verlag, Munich
Typography and design: Horst Erich Wolter, Leipzig · Produced by Druckerei Fortschritt Erfurt
Printed in the German Democratic Republic

LIST OF AUTHORS

*This volume is the joint work of the professional staff
of the Munich Art Galleries and of art historians of the Munich University.
Contributions were made as follows:*

Introduction	Professor Dr. Theodor Müller, Director-General of the Bavarian National Museum
Bavarian State Collections of Paintings *Old Pinakothek* *New Pinakothek* *Schack Gallery* *New State Gallery*	Dr. Hermann Bauer
Collection of Graphic Art	Dr. Dieter Kuhrmann
Bavarian National Museum	Dr. Klaus Maurice
Collections of Classical Art and Glyptothek	Dr. Klaus Vierneisel
Egyptian Collection	Professor Dr. Hans Wolfgang Müller
Residence Museum and Treasury	Director Dr. Hans Thoma
Museum of Ethnology	Director Dr. Andreas Lommel
Coin Collection	Director Dr. Paul Grotemeyer
City Museum	Director Dr. Max Heiss
City Art Gallery in the Lenbach House	Dr. Bernhard Rupprecht

CONTENTS

When between 1568 and 1574 Duke Albrecht V of Bavaria commissioned the Straubing master-turner Jakob Sandtner to construct scale models of the Bavarian ducal towns for his *Kunstkammer*, it shows that he considered the portrayal of these towns to be of such importance that he wanted to preserve a record of their outward appearance at that time for the benefit of future generations. It was the idea that they had a value and characteristic nature all their own which gave rise to the desire to preserve them and to be able to exhibit them with pride. The motive is always a "recognition", that is to say, the recognition of a significance which has to be protected from the ravages of time. Above all the coin and the natural history collections serve to show how easily a perceptive collector comes to desire the completion of a series or group – that is to say, how he seeks to develop a systematic collection.

In addition to these characteristics there grew up during the Age of Enlightenment and after the Declaration of Human Rights another ideal, which was the requirement that these institutions should be an instrument of popular instruction. In 1759 the British Museum in London was created as a public institution. As a result of the revolution the princely collections of art ceased to be a personal privilege. Goethe's "Mouseion" shows a new quality of imagination in which man took prime place. This universalistic conception already foreshadowed in humanism is, it seems to me, most clearly to be seen today in those museums in which objects of social history and of natural science are gathered together under one roof.

And so museums, throughout their history, have undergone a strange and continuous change of character, which can still be seen today in the great variety of the existing institutions: from the chilly hall of fame only to be entered wearing special felt slippers and in which a solemn silence reigns, to the panopticon – and I use this word in no way disparagingly – in which recorded music sounds out from a loudspeaker, tape machines provide explanatory descriptions, and refreshment rooms, smoking lounges and sunlit terraces tempt the visitor to prolong his stay.

It seems to me that Munich was fortunate in that her museums were created at a time when the international consciousness was both enlightened and strong. This has been reflected from their earliest foundations right up to the present day. At the very beginning around 1530 there was the *Lusthaus* of Duke Wilhelm IV. One could wish for no finer beginning. In the recent rearrangement of the Pinakothek it has been possible to bring together again the cycle of historical pictures from this *Lusthaus*, and it is remarkable how, in this setting, even such a unique work of art as Altdorfer's *Battle of Alexander* takes on a new quality.

The oldest document relating to these Wittelsbach art collections is the *Inventarium* of the ducal *Kunstkammer*, which was housed in the upper stories of the building that exists today as the Mint (behind the Central Post Office) and which had been built between 1563 and 1567 as the ducal stables. This *Inventarium* was drawn up by the lawyer J. B. Fickler in 1598. It is a pleasure to be able to identify entries in this inventory of the sixteenth century as works of art which today are on view in, for example, the Residence Museum or the Bavarian National Museum.

The next important stages in the history of the development of the Munich museums can only be touched upon: they comprise the commissions for the priceless gold and crystal works of art of the highest quality made in the late sixteenth and early seventeenth centuries for the Treasury of the Residence; the acquisition in 1613 of Dürer's *Paumgartner Altar* from the Church of St. Catherine in Nuremberg and of the *Four Apostles* by Dürer bought by Elector Maximilian I in 1627 from the Council of the city of Nuremberg; the purchase by Elector Johann Wilhelm of the very fine paintings by Rubens and Rembrandt for the Düsseldorf collection, which was later brought to Munich; and finally the foundation of an ivory and porcelain collection by the Electoral Princes.

In 1805 Dürer's *Self-portrait* was acquired from Nuremberg, and then Ludwig I bought the Boisserée collection, paintings of Perugino and Raphael from Italy, as well as the Aeginetan marbles and the *Barberini Faun*. In 1811 the acquisitions which followed the secularisation of the monasteries came into the *Reiche Kapelle* of the Residence, and the manuscript department of the Bavarian State Library. It would be possible to continue this list indefinitely to show the success with which the activities of the House of Wittelsbach have repeatedly added objects to the subsequent art collections of the Bavarian State which today are famous throughout the world.

The activities of the State Museums that were constituted in the nineteenth century were just as successful. I need only mention as examples the purchase completed in 1853 for the Glyptothek of the *Apollo of Tenea* and the acquisition in 1860, from the collection of Martin von Reider in Bamberg, of the early Christian ivory panel representing Christ's Resurrection, for the Bavarian National Museum. In making these acquisitions the aim was just as much to find works representing the history of the arts in Bavaria and Germany as ones that were of outstanding, world-wide importance. Thus a fine organic picture of artistic contacts developed and it has continued to bear fruit up to the present day.

Without doubt the most splendid gesture to the Europe of the twentieth century was the bequest of Hugo von Tschudi in 1911.

We can also be grateful that again after the Second World War the Munich museums received bequests of outstanding works of art presented from similarly idealistic sentiments. I must mention the bequest of the Preetorius collection in the Ethnological Museum, the Kriss and Reuschel collections in the National Museum, the Gabriele Münter and Bernhard Köhler collections in the City Art Gallery, the Max Fohn collection in the State Collections of Paintings and the Max Kade bequest in the State Collection of Graphic Art. These are all reflections of life and artistic experience. The bequests and presentations too numerous to be mentioned in detail are evidence of the brilliance of our art collections right up to the present day.

It is no less revealing to observe how the rôle of the Munich museums is reflected in the growth of the town.

We may begin our survey with the Residence. We have already mentioned the former *Lusthaus*, the housing of the ducal art collection in the old stable building and the precious objects of the treasuries in the Residence. To that we must add that the entire royal Residence was opened to the public in 1920 as a museum, that in the last war it suffered very considerable damage, and is now in the process of being rebuilt in stages, and re-established as a museum. The Coin Collection founded in 1570 by Duke Albrecht V has also got a new home there.

From the Odeonsplatz a truly royal street, an important architectural creation from the time of Ludwig I, leads to the Greek Gate of the Propylaea built to the plans of Leo von Klenze (1848) on the Königsplatz. On the north side of the Königsplatz is the Glyptothek of Ludwig I (1816), and on the south the former Art Exhibition Building (1838) erected by Georg Friedrich Ziebland. Since this building now houses the State Collections of Classical Art, the square has become an area of classical museums unique in Germany. The beauty and discernment of neo-classic town architecture can be experienced here more purely and forcefully than in almost any other place.

When we add that in the residential quarter which lies in the immediate neighbourhood to the west, Gabriel von Seidl built the studio in the Lenbach villa, where the City Art Gallery was installed between 1927 and 1929, then, I think, the relationship between royal and civic art collecting becomes abundantly clear.

Not far to the north of the Königsplatz lies the square of the Pinakothek buildings, laid out on open land in the Ludovician years of expansion. In the 8 late nineteenth century the area was heavily built over; it suffered great bomb damage during the last war. The New Pinakothek (1853) was completely destroyed. The building of the Old Pinakothek, erected by Leo von Klenze for Ludwig I between 1826 and 1836, after being completely gutted was reconstructed and formally reopened in 1957. It is planned to erect a new building for the State Gallery housing works of the nineteenth and twentieth centuries on the site of the New Pinakothek. When this is done the whole lay-out will fit in with the new buildings that are planned for the State Natural Science Collections on the site of the former Turkish barracks – a splendid project the scope of which extends from classical to modern art.

If we now return to the centre of the old town, we find the Munich City Museum appropriately housed in the noble setting of the late Gothic arsenal and musket-store of the town, which was enlarged a few years ago by a splendid extension, making the way for varied additions in the future.

From the Max-Josephs-Platz in front of the Residence another "royal" street which was laid out by order of Maximilian II in the early second half of the nineteenth century has its starting point; it runs in an eastward direction and led to a crossing of the River Isar. On the far high bank of the Isar the monument of the Maximilianeum was built. Before crossing the river the Maximiliansstrasse widens into an elongated square called the Forum, on the north side of which Bürklein built the Upper Bavarian Government Offices between 1856 and 1859 in the English neo-Gothic "Maximilian style", while on the south side the court architect Riedel erected the Bavarian National Museum between 1858 and 1865. Once again the decidedly national orientation of the museum had led to an appropriate architectural solution.

Within this museum building, the State Ethnological Collection was exhibited after the First World War with particular effect. The building is now being reconstructed following considerable wartime damage. The Preetorius collection, particularly important in the sphere of East Asiatic Art, is on display in an extension building.

Immediately before the First World War Munich once again saw the creation of a similarly impressive roadway, namely the Prinzregentenstrasse on the southern edge of the *Englischer Garten*, parallel to the Maximiliansstrasse. It again was built with the intention of incorporating the farther bank of the Isar in the growing town. Here once again a similar open square was laid out just before the street crossed the river. On its north side is the castle-like building of the new National Museum erected by Gabriel von Seidl in 1900, which was to harmonise with a new building on the south side of the square housing the State Natural Science Collections. But the plan was never carried out, and during the "Third Reich" the bleak building of a District Air Command H.Q. was erected; it is now the Ministry of Commerce. In order to lend the square a special visual quality Adolf von Hildebrand made his Hubertus fountain, which Hitler ordered to be removed – because he disliked it. After the war only Hildebrand's equestrian monument to the Prince Regent was replaced. So there remains no more than a small part of the original plan for this splendid and well thought-out arrangement. But the natural background intended for the plan still remains – the nearby *Englischer Garten*. It must be added that the annexes to the museum have since been used to house the State's Prehistoric Collection and the so-called New Collection, a museum for applied art of modern times.

In the time of the Prince Regent the city buildings spread across the Isar. Munich no longer lay "on the Isar" but became a city through which the Isar flows. It is significant that it was Gabriel von Seidl whom we already know as the creator of the new buildings for the Bavarian National Museum, who starting in 1908 on the so-called *Kohleninsel* in the Isar, directed the construction of the imposing group of buildings known as the *Deutsches Museum*, a museum of the history of Technology and Natural Science.

I wanted to indicate these rings of growth because at the present time, on account of radical reconstruction of the city as a result of the war, they are gradually becoming less obvious. But as the city grows, so places with the most splendid historical castles such as Nymphenburg and Schleissheim which once lay *extra muros*, seem to draw closer.

I hope that in the following monographs it will become clear how the Munich museums form a complete whole while at the same time each bears its own individual stamp.

9

BAVARIAN STATE COLLECTIONS OF PAINTINGS

The Old Pinakothek – it was not until the nineteenth century that the Gallery received this name from Ludwig I – is one of the most beautiful collections in the world. It is significant in two respects, for in addition to the high and indeed often incomparable quality of its paintings, the historical importance of each individual painting bears witness not only to the passion the German princes had for collecting, but also to the particular way in which they fostered art. Just what this amounts to is demonstrated most clearly in the Old Pinakothek in Munich.

This gallery had its beginnings – for it is impossible to speak of its foundation – early in the sixteenth century. Between 1528 and 1530 Duke Wilhelm IV invited the most famous painters of that time in Southern Germany to produce a cycle on the theme of "Heroic acts of great men and women from classical and biblical times", probably for a summer-house at the Residence in Munich. Albrecht Altdorfer's *Battle of Alexander on the River Issus*, which is one of the few examples in the history of painting in miniature which succeeds in achieving monumental effect, rather overshadows in its splendour the other paintings in the series by the artists Hans Burgkmair, the two Jörg Breus, father and son, Barthel Beham, Melchior Feselen, Abraham Schöpfer and Ludwig Refinger. But if each picture is considered separately, it soon becomes obvious that here is a great concept proclaiming the beginning of a new epoch. Three pictures from the series are now in Stockholm, having been carried off by the Swedes in the Thirty Years' War. Here the history of art is inseparably bound up with the political history of the country and of the House of Wittelsbach.

However, the most interesting feature of the series is the fact that in these early days of the princes' zest for collecting, the conception of "antiquity" simply did not exist in art. To Duke Wilhelm a painting was simply an illustration of history, and so everything that he commissioned had direct reference to the Wittelsbach dynasty. Thus the paintings in the cycle for the summer-house had reference to or were examples for the activities of the Renaissance princes, and the series of paintings which Barthel Beham was commissioned to paint contained allusions to the Wittelsbach genealogy. Collecting meant in this sense the immortalising of history in pictures.

During the Renaissance, art was considered principally as a means of exalting history. In later times this view was to some extent overcome, and Duke Albrecht V (1550 to 1579) collected objects of art for the sake of their value. In this mannerist age, "value" meant not simply artistic value, but referred rather to the uniqueness of the artistic achievement which was often almost beyond price. There grew up at this time a princely treasure house of irreplaceable showpieces, and an "antiquarium" for the classical works of art purchased in Italy, amongst which there were also many forgeries. Between 1563 and 1576 the Duke commissioned Wilhelm Egckl to provide a suitable building for his art treasures – the present *Münze* or Mint. The works of art were displayed there indiscriminately mingled with curiosities. There was a Salvator Mundi with "a string by means of which it was possible to move the eyes in the picture", an aborted foetus preserved in spirit, curiosities of nature, precious musk and rare antlers. If this appears incongruous it should be remembered that the modern conception of a work of art, based on middle-class aesthetic attitudes of the nineteenth century, is already beginning to break down. What Albrecht V collected were "objects of art", things artistically and painstakingly

10

wrought of precious material, rarities from classical times or from nature, obtained at great cost and often irreplaceable.

Pictures played their own particular part in this mannerist art collection. On the one hand they were historical documents and therefore valuable; on the other they were "objects of art", documents of artistic achievement bearing witness to the skill of old and contemporary masters in painting, and as such were worthy to be treated as treasures which it was most fitting to lock away in a special chamber, the *Kunstkammer*. This very word tells us much about the manner in which art was considered at that time. Since the work of art had a material value it had to be kept under lock and key. It was to be exhibited only on festive occasions to distinguished guests, but it was very far from being an object of general culture.

In 1583, because of protests made by the provincial diet, Wilhelm V had to discontinue what was termed "the ruinous purchase of strange and useless objects". In any case he took greater pleasure in building than in painting, for his pious nature inclined more towards providing money to found churches than towards acquiring paintings of pagan and mythological themes.

Apart from this, the history of the Munich art collections really begins with Maximilian (1597 to 1651). In the first year of his reign an inventory of the princely art treasures was drawn up, the above-mentioned Fickler inventory. It lists altogether 778 paintings, but of these few can be identified at the present day. In this inventory there was no distinction as yet drawn between objective artistic value and the value of technical accomplishment. But with Maximilian we find a new scale of standards in the princely collections. The Elector as leader of the Counter-reformation, pious without being bigoted, was a political genius just as much as a man obstinate in matters of faith, and brought a new criterion to bear in the collection of paintings, namely that great art was above all suited to portray convincingly the truths of faith if only for the very reason that it was great. It is to Maximilian that we are indebted for the finest and most comprehensive collection of the works by Albrecht Dürer. Perhaps it was because he was fascinated by clarity of form combined with a genuine, profound faith that Maximilian became the leader of a Dürer renais-

sance. In 1630 he acquired the *Paumgartner Altar* from the Church of St. Catherine in Nuremberg, and in 1627 he managed to get from the Nuremberg Council the painting of the *Four Apostles* which had been in the Council Chamber. Much that he acquired is no longer in Munich today; for example, Dürer's painting of *Anna Selbdritt* of 1519 was sold by auction in the nineteenth century, and other paintings were given to Augsburg or Nuremberg. Maximilian tried without success to add Matthias Grünewald's *Isenheim Altar-piece* to his collection. In attempting this, the Elector showed that he had a sure eye for the finest achievements of Old-German painting, in an age when it could by no means be taken for granted.

In going through the Old Pinakothek today the discriminating visitor will find three principal centres of interest in the collection. The first is undoubtedly the incomparable collection of Old-German painting; nowhere else are Dürer, Grünewald and Altdorfer so brilliantly represented. The second is characterised by the name of Rubens, for Munich possesses the largest and probably the finest collection of paintings by the Flemish master that exists, as well as important examples of Dutch and Flemish Baroque painting. The third centre of interest is more difficult to define; and it is the least obvious to anyone who has not studied the history of the collection because it cannot be identified with any one painter or group of painters. It is most easily to be described as an historical phenomenon; the Munich collection is particularly rich in paintings which can best be classified under the general term "devotional paintings". Among these may be mentioned Raphael's paintings of the Madonna, paintings by the Master of the Life of the Virgin, or works of the Cologne or early Dutch schools.

All these paintings were acquired by Ludwig I either from the collection of the Boisserée brothers, or from Italy where a similar concept of art as religious expression existed. This latter group of paintings in the Old Pinakothek which was selected as the result of a partial misunderstanding of late Nazarene views on art, will be examined more closely below.

Each of these three focal points of the collection emerges more or less clearly as the result of a princely concept of art which determined the selection of paintings. It is seen most clearly in the history of the Rubens collection. As early as 1618 Maximilian had in his possession Ruben's *Lion Hunt* as well as three other hunting scenes, and with these he had laid the foundation for the collection. Of the four only the *Lion Hunt* is still in Munich; the *Boar Hunt*, the *Tiger Hunt* and the *Leopard Hunt* were all taken as booty by the French in 1800.

The Elector Ferdinand Maria (1651 to 1679) added scarcely anything to the collection, but in the reign of his successor Max Emanuel (1679 to 1726) there began a period of enthusiastic collecting of Baroque art. Max Emanuel started building a castle at Schleissheim, and its construction was carried on as planned even during the exile of the prince in the War of the Spanish Succession, and to consider this as no more than the product of an absolutist delusion of grandeur, would be to do as little justice to that project as to the plan for an art collection primarily intended to be housed in it. The function of a "picture" was different from that which we consider it to be today. For us a painting from a bygone age is at one and the same time an historical document and a lasting work of art. In the Baroque age a painting was no longer as in the Renaissance a valuable possession to be kept in the treasure house but was something to be shown off, in which a material and artistic value combined to reflect the splendour of its owner.

In 1698 Max II Emanuel bought 105 paintings from Gisbert van Ceulen for 90,000 guilders, part of which he never paid. Amongst them were twelve paintings by Rubens and thirteen by van Dyck. Some of them were presented in 1706 by the Emperor to the Duke of Marlborough during the Austrian occupation, and others were stolen by the French during the Napoleonic Wars, but there remained in Munich a sufficiently large number to constitute the basis of the Rubens collection.

Owing to the fact that van Ceulen had acquired the estate of the Flemish master and subsequently sold it to Munich, the Old Pinakothek possesses a series of private pictures, which when they were painted were never intended for sale. They include the portrait of Hélène Fourment as a mother and many others which had originally been part of Rubens' private collection.

At this time there was still no separate building to house the paintings. They were the property of the princes and adorned the castles in Schleissheim, Nymphenburg and Dachau, the Munich Residence, and the castles in Liechtenberg, Haag, Starnberg, Fürstenried, Laufzorn and so on. Inventories show that though the collection increased in quantity during the reigns of Max Emanuel's successors Karl Albrecht (1726 to 1745) and Max III Joseph (1745 to 1777), no additional works of importance were acquired. In 1775 the Electoral Chancellor and Gallery Director Johann Nepomuk von Weizenfeld published a description of the picture gallery in Schleissheim, and his action was described as "a suitable contribution to the knowledge and dissemination of good taste". Here new aspects of art appreciation are seen to be developing; art has come to be credited with pedagogical value, and it necessarily follows from this that there had to be an attempt to make art treasures accessible to a much wider public.

But before the exclusive collection of the princes was converted into a public museum, it was once again to enjoy the good fortune of a legacy and to suffer the misfortune of being looted.

When the Bavarian line of the House of Wittelsbach came to an end on the death of Max III Joseph, the Elector Palatinate Karl Theodor (1777 to 1799) became master of the Bavarian and Palatinate lands which were united under the terms of the family settlement. Karl Theodor had perforce to take up residence in Munich. This meant that his collections of paintings in Düsseldorf and Mannheim were incorporated into the collection in Bavaria. The paintings from Mannheim were moved to Munich during the lifetime of the Elector, though the Düsseldorf collection was not brought there until 1806.

Karl Theodor's great love for Dutch painting had left its mark on the Mannheim collection. There were more than seven hundred paintings there, most of them small genre-paintings by Steen, Ter Borch, Ostade, Mieris, Dou and others. Before the Mannheim collection was moved to Munich, Karl Theodor had already purchased a considerable number of paintings by Dutch artists for his new residence. They were exhibited together with a number of paintings from the Bavarian collection he had inherited in a new gallery which had been built in 1780 by Lespilliez in the Court garden. Connoisseurs and artists were allowed to enter freely. A new enlightened view of art saw the paintings as an instrument of education, capable "of laying a civilising hand on the people and demonstrating an ennobling influence."

In his book *The Most Distinguished Curiosity of the Capital City Munich*, written in 1788, Rittershausen describes not only the contents of the gallery, but also the life and activities in the Court garden in front of the museum. "Maximilian Joseph allowed young painters to train themselves there and to study according to their needs, and as a result art in Bavaria gained new prestige. It was the wish of Karl Theodor to make the pleasure complete, and in the 79th year of this century the Elector's collection of paintings was transferred to its own appointed building in the Court garden. It rejoices the heart to see a crowd of scholars working there; what delight is felt by everyone who sees the gallery standing open to all men; Theodor could have erected no more worthy monument to art in Bavaria than this..." "The treasures of painting which are kept here are of rare beauty. The finest paintings of the most famous masters are here assembled to delight men of refined taste."

The history of the museum had entered the Age of Enlightenment. It had been recognised that art was intended to provide pleasure to all people, but more important than this was the belief that art was capable of leading the people on through an improved taste to nobler thoughts. The opening of the collections was the culmination of a long process in the history of the museums. The "treasure house" had become, in Rittershausen's words, "a temple to the divine muse who by her art of imitating nature with her brush educates mankind".

The Düsseldorf collection was transferred to Munich not until 1806. Although the inventory contains only 348 items, it was one of the finest collections of Baroque painting. The Elector Wolfgang Wilhelm (1614 to 1635), who was the brother-in-law of Maximilian I, had commissioned a considerable amount of work from Rubens and van Dyck. For example the *Great Last Judgement* was commissioned by him for the Jesuit Church at Neuburg. His grandson Johann Wilhelm (1690 to 1716) had removed the painting from the church and added it to the collection in his gallery in Düsseldorf. Such an action was very typical of this passionate art collector whose judgement and appreciation of quality far eclipsed that of his Bavarian relation Max Emanuel. And it is to him that Munich is indebted for the possession of the most important collection of Rubens' works in the world. Above all with the dowry of his wife Maria Loisia de'Medici he purchased the *Small Last Judgement, Christ and the Penitent Sinners*, the *Madonna in the Flower Garland*, the *Rape of the Daughters of Leucippus*, the *Crowning of the Hero of Virtue* and the *Artist and his Wife in the Honey-suckle Bower*, and these were but a few of his finest acquisitions. There were also paintings by van Dyck, Jordaens, and Steen, as well as Rembrandt's cycle of paintings of the Passion. From his wife he received Raphael's *Canigiani Holy Family* as a wedding gift. Jan Willem sent out agents who travelled throughout all Europe in search of outstanding works of art, and it is significant that they were directed to spend the whole sum of money which they had at their disposal on a single work, rather than on several minor ones. In 1806 the Düsseldorf collection was moved to Munich, although a protracted lawsuit with Prussia over Bavaria's rights of inheritance dragged on until 1870.

Karl Theodor's successor, Max IV Joseph (1799 to 1825), came from the Pfalz-Zweibrücken line of the House of Wittelsbach. Thus the paintings from Zweibrücken also went to Munich. This collection consisted principally of pictures which Duke Karl August had purchased from his Court painter Christian von Mannlich. In his memoirs Mannlich describes graphically how they succeeded in saving the collection from the approaching French. "The general, whose name I have forgotten ... had the gallery opened up. He strode unhurriedly through the first room, which he found empty, and when he discovered that there was just as little in the following rooms he said angrily, 'Damn it, there is nothing here!' 'What has happened to the pictures?' he asked impatiently. 'They have been taken to Munich which is where they were intended for. You have seized nothing but empty rooms ...'"

The years which followed were full of adventure. Hardly had an inventory of the collection in Munich been drawn up, and the paintings distributed between the gallery in the Court garden and those at Schleissheim and Nymphenburg when a French attack was also threatening there. Since 1790 the painter Johann Georg Dillis had been in charge of the gallery. In 1800 he found it necessary to remove a number of the most important paintings to Ansbach for safe keeping. But it is first and foremost to 13

Mannlich, who from 1799 was the head of the central administration of the Bavarian art collection, that we are indebted for the preservation of the art treasures through these difficult years. It was through no fault of his that during the occupation of Munich General Le Courbe took paintings from the Residence. "Soon after this shock I was to suffer yet another, far more disastrous than the first," he writes. "One fine morning an elegantly attired 'Citizen' wearing a fine blond wig dressed à la Titus entered my room. Having asked me if I were the Director of the Electoral Museums he continued: 'I am the Commissary of the Rhine Army and am authorised by the Republic to increase our own riches by the booty obtained from the conquered nations, in making a selection from their rich collections of artistic and scientific treasures!'" In the end Commissary Neveu carried off seventy-two paintings amongst which was Altdorfer's *Battle of Alexander*, destined to adorn Napoleon's bathroom, as well as Titian's *Crowning with Thorns* and Rubens' *Meleager and Atalante*. A reciprocal bond was given promising compensation in the form of works by French masters. It was never honoured, which is quite in keeping with the tragicomic turn the whole affair was to take. "When the king returned to the French throne in 1814, I handed over my papers to Professor Thiersch who had been sent from our Court to Paris to reclaim our works of art. But the Monarchy showed itself just as little inclined to restitution as the Republic before it ... Soon after this the authorities with almost incredible irresponsibility relinquished their claim to the treasures of which they had been deprived in this way. Herr Thiersch returned with empty hands, and when the following year the Allies once again marched victoriously into Paris, they restored to us only forty-eight out of the seventy-two pictures." Dillis had in any case advised that the claim to some of the pictures should be waived, since the cost of their recovery would be too great. Thus three of the hunting scenes by Rubens, Tintoretto's *Madonna with Saints* and several magnificent Dutch paintings remained in France.

The legacy from Zweibrücken was the last addition of its kind. In scarcely any other collection is the genealogy of its ruling house reflected to such a degree, and the student of history will find on walking through the Old Pinakothek that these links are abundantly clear.

In the secularisation of 1803, the ecclesiastical estates in Bavaria and the Tyrol, which at that time was Bavarian, were dissolved. The dispossession of church property left an immense number of works of art unhoused. Much was destroyed through ignorance; even more was squandered. Mannlich sought to save what he could. He writes bitterly of an arduous journey through the whole of Bavaria: "My journey had lasted for two months, and would have been less wearisome if the possessions had still been within the monasteries ... We had to seek lodging in the vilest of taverns, where previously only carriers and draymen would spend the night. Everything was disgustingly filthy, the beds, table-cloths and napkins and no less the wretched food which never failed to nauseate us. I returned to Munich with a rich harvest of fine paintings snatched from the hands of barbarians." After this journey through Bavaria he brought back with him Holbein's *Wettenhausen Altar-piece*, the panels portraying the *Life of the Virgin* from Kaisheim, Wolf Huber's *Scenes from the Passion* from Passau, Pacher's *Altar-piece of the Church Fathers* from Neustift near Brixen, Grünewald's *Saints Erasmus and Maurice* from Aschaffenburg, the High-altar by Rubens from Freising and Tiepolo's *Adoration of the Magi* from Münsterschwarzach. But his greatest pride was the acquisition of a supposed Raphael which subsequently proved to be "no more" than the work of a master painter from Upper Italy.

Von Mannlich was a classicist. It was only after his death, in the time of his successor, Johann Georg von Dillis, that the so-called "primitives", the early Italian painters, the Dutch artists of the 15th century and the Old-German artists, were to receive the recognition that they deserved. But it was the Crown Prince, later King Ludwig I, who had the most decisive influence on the collection. Already in 1805 he had presented Giotto's *Last Supper* to the gallery. His greatest contribution was undoubtedly made when he bought the collection owned by the Boisserée brothers (1827) and so brought to Munich the finest collection of early German and Dutch paintings, which had already been much admired by Goethe. "What a collection I have got now, gentlemen. What a collection, when all are brought together!" His exclamation of pride was justified. Amongst the many outstanding works of art which now came to Munich were Rogier van der Weyden's altar-piece from the Church of St. Columba in Cologne, Dirck Bouts' *Pearl of Brabant*, the painting *Saint Veronica with the Holy Kerchief* by a master of the Cologne school, and altar-pieces by Stephan Lochner. "I only hope that nothing of all this appears in the newspapers, and in particular that they do not learn the price I paid. If I lose money on gambling or spend it on horses people are prepared to accept it as right and inevitable; but if I spend it on art they begin to talk of extravagance."

In the next year Ludwig acquired the collection of Prince Wallerstein, which included outstanding panels by Upper German and Swabian painters. With these additions the Munich gallery's collection became the most important in existence for early German painting.

While the Romantic view of art had regarded Dürer and Raphael as kindred spirits, it was Ludwig who actually brought the two together in a most harmonious way in his collection. His emissaries managed to acquire Raphael's *Madonna della Tenda*, and two outstanding works in the Wallerstein collection were Dürer's *Oswolt Krel* and Altdorfer's *Danube Landscape*.

In 1822 Dillis began to draw up a comprehensive inventory of the paintings, and in the same year plans were discussed for the construction of a new museum as the building in the Court garden was no longer large enough. In the end the king commissioned Leo von Klenze to draw up the plans, and by 1826 they had progressed to such an extent that the foundation-stone could be laid on 7th April, the date of Raphael's birth. Ten years later, on 16th October 1836, the Old Pinakothek was opened to the public.

Dillis was able to announce to the king, "Magnificent and without parallel this precious monument stands now complete as a most eloquent witness of Your Royal Highness' deep and fervent love of art." And the building on the Barerstrasse standing in its setting of green lawns is indeed one of the most successful museum buildings of the 19th century. It is the happy outcome of mature deliberation, although there existed scarcely any earlier examples from which to draw inspiration. In order to get lighting from above, since window lighting was to be used only in the smaller rooms, the three parts of the main building were set in an east-west direction with projecting corner wings; the south side

formed the main façade. A loggia entrance on this side made it possible to enter each room separately. Historically the building is a very early example of the use of Italian Renaissance forms in German classicism. This was deliberately done; it was intended as a monument to the Renaissance as the cradle of the arts. Inspired by Raphael's loggias in the Vatican, the king wanted to adorn the loggias of his building with pictures representing the history of painting. A "journey through the history of art" in the form of historical and allegorical paintings executed by Clemens Zimmermann from sketches by Cornelius was to introduce and conclude the educational tour of the collection. The central piece was an allegory of religion served by the arts. In addition there were paintings celebrating the beginnings of Germanic culture under Charlemagne, German architecture in the 13th century, the Cologne school of painters, the works of the van Eyck brothers, and those of Memling, Lucas van Leyden, Holbein and Dürer. Similar loggia paintings were dedicated to Claude Lorrain, Rembrandt, Poussin, Le Sueur and Rubens and in particular to Raphael, Michelangelo, the Venetian artists, Correggio, Leonardo and Perugino, as well as to Fra Angelico, Giotto and Cimabue. Legends from the lives of the artists, anecdotes and historical events were combined in a spiritualistic and at the same time naive view of the history of art. There are names which mean little to us today. But at the same time there is an admirable idealist view of the totality of an historical movement in which, by illustrating the achievements of the past, the present is given its high aims.

However, the most remarkable feature of the building was that when it was built the king considered his collection already complete. His goal had been reached. The building was designed around the pictures, and each room was intended from the outset for specific pictures. This was possible since the paintings were considered as documents of man's history.

Although Ludwig added new palatial façades to his old Residence, it is true to say that the days of monumental palace architecture were past. The representative function of architecture was transferred from palaces to public buildings with a cultural purpose: theatres and museums. Evidence of this is the furnishing of the rooms. Stucco and silk-damask

15

tapestries previously found in princely halls, now adorned a palace of art.

When the galleries were opened to the public on 16th October 1836, Munich possessed one of the earliest and finest museum buildings in Germany.

In 1944 the building was almost completely destroyed by bombs. It was possible to rebuild it but so far funds have not been available for a complete restoration of the exterior. The interior has been restored, although through the re-siting of the great staircase and other alterations much of the earlier magnificence of the building has been lost. On 7th June 1957 the Pinakothek was reopened, after its principal works of art had been on exhibition for some time in the *Haus der Kunst*. In rooms on the ground floor which had originally housed the collection of classical vases, the collection of engravings and the collection of painted porcelain, a new section was created in the east wing for "German and Dutch painting from Renaissance to Baroque", and parts of the collection of Old-German painting were housed in the west wing.

After the abdication of King Ludwig and the death of Johann Georg von Dillis in 1841, the position of director became no more than a "refuge for professors of art in their old age". Dilettanti auctioned off valuable pictures and bunglers made inexpert attempts at restoring paintings. It was only in 1875 on the nomination of Franz von Rebers to the position of director of the gallery that a real expert was once again in charge. In 1884, in collaboration with Adolf Bayersdorfer, he produced the first official catalogue. At this time also some new acquisitions of importance were made, including Leonardo's *Madonna*, Signorelli's *Madonna Tondo* and Antonello's *Virgin of the Annunciation*.

In 1909 Hugo von Tschudi was nominated as director of the State Galleries in Bavaria. Although his greatest services were in the acquisition of modern painting, his fine feeling for quality guided him both to prune the collection and to bring into prominence what was of true value. The number of paintings on exhibition was reduced but this time nothing was squandered. Several outstanding paintings were purchased: Greco's *Disrobing of Christ* and Guardi's *Venetian Gala Concert* as well as Goya's *Plucked Turkey, Frying-pan and Herrings*. After the early death of Tschudi in 1911, H. Braune held the position temporarily until 1914 when Friedrich Dörnhöffer became director of the newly named Bavarian State Collections of Paintings. The years of expansion were long past as rising prices limited the extent of new acquisitions. Nevertheless, amongst those that were added there was a fine Strigel, Amberger's *Christoph Fugger*, Brueghel's *The Land of Cockayne* and Tintoretto's *Mars and Venus*. The director's main task was, however, in the sphere of restoration and preservation of the paintings already in the gallery.

When in 1933 the distinguished authority on Old-German painting, Ernst Buchner, succeeded Dörnhöffer in office, the political thunder clouds were already gathering which finally led to the catastrophe of 1945. If Ernst Buchner had written his memoirs, as Mannlich had done, a great portion of them would certainly have been devoted to the story of the concealment and ultimate recovery of the collections from the State Galleries. After the war Eberhard Hanfstaengl took over the collection, and finally it was granted to Buchner not only to direct the reconstruction of the Old Pinakothek but to see the plans realised. His successor Kurt Martin was in charge of the collection until 1964. He, and since 1964 Halldor Soehner, have succeeded in making this "palace" of art into a living museum, attracting each year a growing number of enthusiastic visitors.

NEW PINAKOTHEK

With the completion of the Old Pinakothek King Ludwig I of Bavaria had housed the art of earlier days in a "palace" which at the same time – and this appears to some extent paradoxical – was to make this same art accessible to the public. Already in the fourth decade of that century he had decided to erect a similar building for contemporary works of art, and on 12th October 1846 the foundation-stone was laid. "The New Pinakothek is intended to house paintings of this and future centuries. The higher art of painting had died out, to arise again in the nineteenth century with the Germans, like a Phoenix from the ashes, and not only the art of painting but all the visual arts were recreated in new splendour.

Art cannot be considered as a luxury; it shall express itself in all things; it shall merge into life and only then is it what it should be. My great artists are my pride and joy. The work of the politician will long have passed away while that of the consummate artist continues to delight and inspire."

In these moving sentences from the inaugural address we hear an echo of Schiller's ideas in his "Letters on the Aesthetic Culture of Man" in which he expressed the conviction that art can survive the decline of history. Ludwig's speech was prophetic. Soon he was forced to give up his throne. But his art collection too outlived history only partially. During the Second World War August von Voit's building with the frescoes by Wilhelm von Kaulbach was completely destroyed. One of the frescoes showed Ludwig surrounded by artists and scholars. This picture too was destroyed with the building. What remained was a collection of art of the nineteenth century which the king believed to be the beginnings of a new art which could rise to new heights as in the days of the Renaissance.

When the New Pinakothek was opened in 1853, much was no more than planned and expressed in the frescoes by Kaulbach; the walls of the new building were but sparsely adorned with works of art. Today the building has disappeared and only the paintings are left, to bear witness to a programme for art determined by high ideals and aims.

In accordance with this plan the New Pinakothek was intended for paintings which "did not date from earlier than this century", that is, it was to be an art collection of the nineteenth century. When the building became the property of the State in 1915, the rooms had become so crowded that it was necessary to rearrange them and to make certain structural modifications. This was because since the eighties the State itself had been active in the purchase of paintings especially from the annual exhibitions of contemporary art in Munich, and each time these paintings were added with increasing difficulty to those already in the building on the Barerstrasse. Ultimately the overcrowding became such that it was necessary to create a modern section out of the New Pinakothek's collection, and this became the New State Gallery.

This measure had the same effect as that which Ludwig I had once achieved in his separation of the Pinakothek into the Old and the New: the past became a closed chapter of history, from which contemporary art was once again separated. The result was a special museum for the earlier art of the nineteenth century. And so Ludwig's endeavour to encourage contemporary art became itself a matter of art history preserved in the museum. Contemporary art made a fresh beginning.

On looking through the first catalogues of the New Pinakothek from 1853 and 1868, there appear more names of artists who today have been forgotten than of those who have survived the transition to modern times. But in order to reconstruct the original appearance of the collection and its plan of development we must take into consideration those pictures which in the meantime have fallen victim to the passage of history.

Although today the finest paintings of the New Pinakothek together with those of the New State Gallery are temporarily housed in the *Haus der Kunst*, the old catalogues of the collection reveal a system in the distribution and selection of the pictures in the former New Pinakothek in which Ludwig's aims are clear to see.

We are reminded of the king's journeys to Rome in 1804 and 1818, and of the German-Roman circle of artists which included Koch, Reinhart, Hess, Overbeck and Catel. Many of the finest paintings of the collection are by these artists, who, although they differ in style and theme, were at that time united with the young king in pursuit of a high ideal.

The New Pinakothek had very spacious rooms capable of housing the largest of paintings, such as programme art and huge historical canvases. Carl Piloty's *Seni before the Corpse of Wallenstein* and his *Thusnelda* are probably the most popular examples of this genre, which is derived principally from the Dutch-Belgian school. These historical paintings are clearly didactic in purpose and just as clearly they are intended to glorify their royal patron. The sketches in oil by Kaulbach for the external frescoes of the New Pinakothek were exhibited in a separate room. The picture by Franz Catel of the visit of Crown Prince Ludwig to the Spanish wine-house in Rome is now a document of social history. In a separate room 23 representations of Greek landscapes were on exhibition, which the king commissioned Karl Rottmann to paint between 1836 and 1850. In the principal of these, *Nemea*, "King Ludwig I 17 is seen, surrounded by Greeks who, bearing palm branches in their hands, do homage to him". These striking examples of neo-classic-romantic landscape painting are a reference to the link between Greece and Bavaria and to the artistic discovery of the Greek landscape. In two vast pictures Peter von Hess illustrated the arrival in Nauplia on 6th February 1833 of the Greek King Otto, the second son of Ludwig, and his entry into Athens.

The general impression which the New Pinakothek originally made was to no small extent determined by a discrepancy which existed between the artistic capabilities and the elevated and ambitious themes. A further discrepancy lay in the sharp contrast between the large-scale official paintings in the main rooms and the small-scale and genre paintings pushed away in the small side-rooms. Thus the original collection was in a large measure an illustration of the growing gulf in the nineteenth century between the subjects commissioned and the level of artistic accomplishment.

Today the collection presents a considerably altered picture. At the beginning of the century the contents of the gallery were examined and more than 350 paintings withdrawn from exhibition. In their place, works from the late 18th and early 19th centuries were added and in this way a boundary line was drawn between the Old and New Pinakothek, which represents the division between Baroque and more recent times.

Some of the finest paintings in the collection are purchases which were made at the turn of the century and before the reorganisation of the collection in 1915. Although Ludwig himself had bought nothing by Schwind, the *Symphony* came to the gallery as part of the estate of King Otto, and in 1900 the fine sketches for the murals in the Vienna Opera House were acquired. Böcklin's *Pan among the Reeds* of 1857 was purchased as early as 1859, but his *Idyll* and *Play of the Waves* were not added to the collection until much later. Although the paintings by Feuerbach, and in particular his *Medea* of 1870, fit very well stylistically into the general character of the collection, its coherence was almost shattered by the addition of the most important paintings by Hans von Marées as the bequest of Dr. Fiedler.

A new age was beginning with a new art. When the second catalogue of the New Pinakothek appeared there was a group of painters in Paris who were not at first taken seriously, but who nevertheless were soon to revolutionise painting. They called themselves "Impressionists". That Munich today houses some of the major works of these Impressionists presupposed that a new collection was formed and that the New Pinakothek took its place in history.

SCHACK GALLERY

The least known part of the Bavarian State Collections of Paintings is probably the Schack Gallery which since 1909 has been housed in a building of its own in the Prinzregentenstrasse. However, some of the finest pictures from the former private collection of Count Schack are today numbered among the possessions of the New Pinakothek.

The history of this collection is not without its lighter moments. The founder of the collection and the most important patron of contemporary art, and in particular of South German painting, was a Mecklenburg junker who during his lifetime had but little contact with the town in which his gallery was to find its home. Adolf Friedrich, Baron and later Count von Schack, born in Brüsewitz near Schwerin in 1815 as the son of a member of the Assembly of the German Diet, was something of a rare phenomenon in Munich, being reminiscent rather of the generally accepted picture of the widely cultured English gentleman-traveller. In the course of his studies in Law he became acquainted with almost all the large towns of Germany, and even by his twenties extensive travels had taken him to Italy, Spain, Greece and the Near East. He dabbled in literature and wrote mediocre poetry, which was soon forgotten, but at the same time he was so conscious of his own limitations that he deliberately turned his love of art to a different purpose, namely to the encouragement of painters whose genius had remained unappreciated. Nevertheless it was his translation of the Persian poet Firdusi which first drew upon him the attention of King Max of Bavaria and led to his being summoned to Munich. As a result of his *History of Dramatic Literature and*

Art in Spain he was made a member of the Order of Maximilian in 1854, and in 1856 honorary member of the Bavarian Academy of Science. From 1857 he lived in Munich, but he was just as much at home in Florence and Rome.

As he himself wrote later in his book *My Collection of Paintings*, his lack of literary success wounded him so deeply that for this very reason he decided to devote himself to the care of neglected talents, a behaviour pattern which the psychologists would label "compensation". The cosmopolitan Schack was equally an admirer of Italian Renaissance painting and a nationalist as far as modern art was concerned. The result of this duality was that on the one hand he was the first to plan anything in the nature of an ideal museum, and on the other hand he wanted to help contemporary German art, which at that time was dominated by art of other countries, to assume once again its rightful place.

In the course of making his collection he commissioned to this end 85 copies of Old Masters to be carried out by Lenbach, Lipphart, Wolff and Marées. "The finest contribution that a king could make to the art of his country would be a museum in which were to be found excellent copies of all the principal works of art scattered throughout the world."

More important than such schemes was his encouragement of unrecognised or generally underestimated talents. He was not poor, but also not rich enough to be able to make unlimited purchases. On one occasion it was even necessary for the king to place at his disposal 60,000 guilders so that Schack should be able to continue to fill his house in the Briennerstrasse. Often enough the artists would complain of his lack of generosity, but this stemmed entirely from a discrepancy between the extent of his financial resources and the calls made upon them.

"If I have succeeded in removing the curse of neglect under which Germany has permitted so many of her best sons to languish, from only one misjudged genius, then in my last hour I shall be able to say that I have not lived in vain." The first painter whom he tried to rescue from the shadows of neglect by providing commissions, was Bonaventura Genelli. He was already sixty years old and poor when Schack first met him, and as examples of his work could produce only sketches and no substantial oil paintings. When Schack commissioned paintings from him he had to learn the technique of colour over again from the beginning. The result seen objectively from the more distant viewpoint of today was a fiasco. The "genius" of Genelli failed precisely in the working out of his sketches. A glib and often painfully naturalistic technique destroyed the promise of genius.

Schack's greatest contribution was the large number of works he commissioned from Moritz von Schwind. Thirty-three of his pictures give us today a cross-section of his artistic development up to his death in 1871. "When we stand before his creations, it is as if we could breathe in the very air of the German oak forests; hunting horns ring out to us from amongst the trees; distant hilltops crowned with ancient castles gleam in the sunlight; in the gorges gnomes dwell; fairies float in the mists of morning. A magical light spreads over everything, a rosy dawn recalling the days of our earliest childhood." Thus the art of Moritz von Schwind is sympathetically described in the book by Schack, through whose patronage it is better represented in Munich than anywhere else. The works of Eduard Steinle and Joseph von Führich pale in comparison because of their frequently exaggerated sentimentality.

In 1862 on the occasion of an exhibition Schack's attention was drawn to Anselm von Feuerbach, for whom he secured several commissions in the following years. In 1859 he had met Arnold Böcklin in Munich. He found in his pictures "that ineffable charm which only a genius can bestow on a picture. To attempt to demonstrate this to someone who does not feel it for himself would indeed be in vain." The discovery of the humour of Karl Spitzweg does credit to Schack with his romantic classicism. Spitzweg's pictures are "equally filled with humour and with deep and sensitive feeling, and their artistic execution too leaves nothing to be desired".

Within the rather gloomy rooms of the Schack Gallery, which are nevertheless well suited to the pictures they house, we discover examples of an art which has largely passed into oblivion, the very oblivion from which Schack wanted to save it. Many of them did not survive the critical judgement of later generations and became no more than a record of idealistic collecting. But there was in fact much real treasure hitherto unrecognised which Schack brought into prominence. Of his own critical judgement he writes: "If I were to rely on it to any extent at all, 19

I could not hide from myself the possibility of mistakes and deceptions, but I would prefer to be led into error by my own opinions independently than by the masses." Earlier a great part of the artistic public had bestowed its boundless admiration on such artists as Defregger, Kaulbach, Makart and Piloty. Schack felt that he himself had been underestimated, so now he wanted to help neglected artists, and in fact in many cases these artists proved to have been most unfairly wronged.

For the presence of this collection today in the State of Bavaria we are indebted to Emperor Wilhelm II – and this is a rather curious facet of the history of the Schack Gallery. During his lifetime Schack offered the collection to the city of Munich as a legacy, but Munich refused the bequest. And so on Schack's death in 1894 the collection passed to Prussia. The Emperor, however, allowed it to remain in Munich, and when in 1909 the Prussian Embassy was built on the Prinzregentenstrasse, special rooms were furnished in it to receive the Schack collection. The works of the artists whom Schack had encouraged are now in this same house, systematically arranged and grouped into Late Romanticists, Neo-classic painters and Idyllic painters. The copies no longer hold any interest.

NEW STATE GALLERY

The New State Gallery, like the Old and the New Pinakothek and the Schack Gallery, forms a part of the Bavarian State Collections of Paintings and comprises according to the preface in the catalogue of 1920, the State's collection of modern paintings and sculpture. In other words, the New State Gallery is that part of the State Collections in Munich which is continually changing and which will grow through the acquisition of contemporary works of art, so that in time some items will have to be removed to storage, just as they were in the New Pinakothek. Again as in the case of the New Pinakothek it may even one day become necessary to declare the collection complete, because a phase of art, once modern, has meanwhile moved into history. Already the collection of Impressionist art in the New State Gallery constitutes a unit within clearly defined limits, and it is unlikely to change to any extent.

The problems which arise in directing a growing collection of modern art are different from those of, let us say, the Old Pinakothek. For here time puts to the test, swiftly and without mercy, the critical judgement and feeling for quality of those whose task it is to select from the immense output of modern art those items which may hope to survive the verdict of time and history.

The sort of difficulties which can arise are exemplified in the case of Hugo von Tschudi, who made sweeping changes in the State art collections. Tschudi was at first director of the National Gallery in Berlin. His progressive attitude and his choice of acquisitions, which today are numbered among the pearls of the collection, led to many conflicts and to an open quarrel in the presence of the Emperor. An impossible situation was resolved when Tschudi was summoned to Munich in 1909. The first thing he did was to carry out the re-hanging of the pictures in the Old Pinakothek, the first in modern times. There was also talk of his purchases of old paintings.

Even more important were his attempts through the acquisition of modern paintings to associate himself with a development which was threatening to by-pass Germany, for in the meantime a new era in Western painting had begun in France. As he had done in Berlin, Tschudi now sought in Munich to acquire masterpieces of the Impressionists and the Post-Impressionists. He wanted "a platform of German and also French art of the nineteenth century in the Old Pinakothek. Freed from local and political interests, raised high above the commonplace, the masterpieces, closely linked by their quality alone to the great works of earlier centuries, were to uphold the historical traditions and at the same time give assurance to the coming generations." It is not surprising that Tschudi, by his high praise of French art, made himself unpopular in art circles in Munich. When in 1910 he walked in silence through the Crystal Palace Exhibition and declared afterwards that he had found nothing there worth buying, protests were made to the Prince Regent and to the Minister, just as they had previously been made in Berlin to the Emperor, demanding Tschudi's dismissal. But Tschudi was already suffering from a fatal illness, from which he died in 1911.

At this time there was a number of pictures by the French Impressionists in the store-rooms of the museum which Tschudi hoped would be presented by patrons or acquired by the State. The task of executing Tschudi's will fell to his successor Heinz Braune, and he instituted the idea of the "Tschudi bequest" by which the means were sought to enable the acquisitions to be made. The foundation-stone of the bequest was Manet's *Breakfast in the Studio* presented by a Starnberg business-man. Then in 1912 the State bought Monet's *Bridge over the Seine at Argenteuil*, and subsequently a whole series of paintings were acquired which included Cézanne's *Railway Cutting, Still Life*, and *Self-portrait*, Gauguin's *Composition from Tahiti*, van Gogh's *View of Arles* and his *Sunflowers*. As far back as 1910 an art dealer had agreed to reserve for Tschudi the opportunity to buy Manet's *The Boat*; the purchase was not completed until 1914, and this was the last acquisition made by the Tschudi bequest.

Since almost all the purchases were made possible by private gifts, the State finally gave its approval to the new artistic policy. But in a ministerial decree of 1912 it pointed out that the Ministry reserved the right to decide whether the paintings would in fact be incorporated in the collection. Today they make the New State Gallery into one of the finest museums of French painting. By acquisitions made up to 1929 and then again after 1950, the collection has been systematically enlarged. From Delacroix and Géricault to Corot and on to Impressionism and Post-Impressionism, from Cézanne and van Gogh to Picasso, Braque and Matisse, the development of modern painting is illustrated in a few, but without exception, outstanding examples. Cézanne's *Railway Cutting*, van Gogh's *Sunflowers* and Manet's *Breakfast in the Studio* have become so popular that it is not necessary to emphasise them. Alongside them the visitor can discover numbers of less familiar pictures which are equally worthy of his admiration: Sisley's *Street near Hampton Court* perhaps or Pissarro's *Street in Upper Norwood*, Renoir's *Landscape with View of the Sacré Cœur*, a late work by Cézanne, the *Bend in a Road*, or Bonnard's *After the Bath*.

Recently a number of purchases have been made which not only, in their excellent quality, can take their place alongside the pictures of the Tschudi bequest, but which also represent a valuable supplement to it. Degas' *Henri Rouart and his Son* is a splendid example of French portrait painting. Braque's *La Calanque – temps gris* and particularly Picasso's *Madame Soler* of 1903 mark the movement towards the art of the twentieth century.

The brilliance of the French paintings all too easily blinds us to the fine achievements of the contemporary German movements. The late Romantic Taunus landscapes of Hans Thomas, Wilhelm Trübner's Impressionist portraits, Liebermann's *Old Woman with Goats* and particularly Wilhelm Leibl's portraits of women (Fräulein Kirchdorffer and Frau Gedon) all show that Germany at this time was doing more than merely treading well-worn paths.

The work of an Italian Impressionist and of the foremost Swiss painter at the turn of the century is represented in Munich by Segantini's *Ploughing in the Engadine*, and by Hodler's *Weary of Life* and his study for a *Fighter for Freedom*.

After French Impressionist painting, German Expressionism forms the largest section in the New State Gallery. This is not as self-evident as it at first appears. After it had been proscribed by the "Third Reich" as degenerate and therefore banished from the State collection, one of those post-war miracles was necessary to reassemble items which today form a large part of the collection. After 1945 Eberhard Hanfstaengl had begun with modest means to acquire works by Franz Marc and particularly by artists of the *Brücke* group. Finally in 1965 the New State Gallery received an unusual bequest, the largest since the Tschudi bequest. In 1937, after an exhibition of "Degenerate Art", Goebbels had the paintings which had been torn from the collections stored in Berlin, so that they might later be publicly burned or sold. The painters, Emanuel Fohn and his wife Sofie, who were living in Rome at this time, owned a fine collection of Romantic art. They sacrificed this, for the sake of saving what was left to save of those paintings in Berlin. Among the pictures were Macke's *Girl under Trees*, Jawlensky's *Elongated Head in Brownish-red*, Marc's *Mandrill*, Kokoschka's *Emigrant*, Corinth's *Walchensee, with Mountains in Clouds* and Beckmann's *Large Still Life with Telescope*. In 1965 the Fohn bequest passed to Munich. It consists of 16 paintings and more than 100 sketches and water-colours. Since then it has been possible to make good the most serious 21 omissions so that today German Expressionism is once again outstandingly well represented.

All the painters of the *Blaue Reiter* and the *Brücke* groups are represented by at least one example, as well as the Constructivists of the Bauhaus including Schlemmer, and the prophets of non-representational painting from Kandinsky and Klee to their most recent followers Soulages, Werner and Nay. We cannot yet know how the collection, or rather the exhibition from this collection will appear in fifty year's time and what choices time will have made from amongst the acquisitions of today.

The Bavarian State Collections of Paintings include no works of sculpture associated with its older sections. Since the Bavarian National Museum is no longer "responsible" for modern art, the State Gallery has taken modern sculpture in its charge. Today only a few pieces are on exhibition, but amongst them are outstanding works of the most important masters, such as Rodin's *Crouching Woman* and *Eva*, Maillol's *Standing Youth* and *Flora*, Archipenko's *Boxers*, Marini's *Miracolo* and Moore's *Fallen Warrior*. Of particular interest are some works of sculpture by painters, such as Matisse's *Slave*, Picasso's *Fernande*, Schlemmer's *Abstract Figure* and Beckmann's *Man in Darkness*.

After its separation from the New Pinakothek, the New State Gallery was housed in Ziebland's Art Exhibition Building of 1838 on the Königsplatz. Since the end of the war the collection has found temporary accommodation in the west wing of the *Haus der Kunst*.

DESCRIPTION OF ILLUSTRATIONS

3 Stephan Lochner. Born about 1410, probably in Meersburg (on Lake Constance), died in Cologne 1451. *Adoration of the Christ Child*. On oak, 36 × 23 cm. About 1445. Transferred from the possession of the State in 1961. AP No. 13169

4/5 Michael Pacher. Born about 1435, probably in Bruneck (in the Pustertal), died 1498 in Salzburg. *Altar-piece of the Church Fathers*. On pine; centre panel, left side (St. Augustine) 212 × 100 cm., centre panel, right side (St. Gregory) 212 × 100 cm.; left wing (St. Jerome) 216 × 91 cm.; right wing (St. Ambrose) 216 × 91 cm. Painted between 1467 and 1483. The altar with its wings closed shows scenes from the legend of St. Wolfgang. Acquired 1812 from the Augustine Convent of Neustift near Brixen. AP No. 2597–2600

6 Albrecht Altdorfer. Born 1480, probably in Regensburg, died there 1538. *Leafy Wood with Saint George*. Parchment on lime, 28.2 × 22.5 cm. Signed with the monogram AA and the date 1510. From the Boisserée collection. AP No. WAF 29

7 Lucas Cranach the Elder. Born 1472 in Kronach (Upper Franconia), died in Weimar 1553. *Cardinal Albrecht von Brandenburg in Prayer before a Crucifix*. On pine, 158 × 112 cm. Painted about 1520–25. Purchased in 1829 from the Stiftskirche in Aschaffenburg. AP No. 3819

8 Albrecht Dürer. Born 1471 in Nuremberg, died there 1528. *Self-portrait in a Fur Coat*. On lime, 67 × 49 cm. Signed with the date 1500 and the monogram AD. An inscription defines the portrait as a self-portrait of Dürer at the age of 28. Bought in Nuremberg 1805. AP No. 537

9 Altdorfer. *The Victory of Alexander the Great over Darius in the Battle on the River Issus*. On lime, 158.4 × 120.3 cm. (cut on all the sides). Framed inscription names Albrecht Altdorfer. In addition monogram AA and date 1529. Belonged to a cycle of historical paintings commissioned by Duke Wilhelm IV. AP No. 688

10 a) Dürer. *The Paumgartner Altar*. On lime; centre panel (the Birth of Christ) 155 × 126 cm.; left wing (Saint George = Stephan Paumgartner) 157 × 61 cm.; right wing (Saint Eustace = Lukas Paumgartner) 157 × 61 cm. Centre panel signed with monogram AD. Painted about 1500. Acquired by Maximilian I from the Church of St. Catherine in Nuremberg. AP Nos. 706, 701, 702

10 b) Dürer. *Centre Panel of the Paumgartner Altar*

11 Dürer. *Lamentation*. On pine, 151 × 121 cm. Presented by Albrecht Glimm; painted about 1500. Probably acquired by Maximilian I. AP No. 704

12 Mathis Gothart-Neithart, called Grünewald. Born about 1460 in Würzburg, died 1528 in Halle. *Saints Erasmus and Maurice*. On lime, 226 × 176 cm. Painted about 1520 for the New Collegiate Church of St. Maurice and St. Mary Magdalene in Halle. Acquired 1836. AP No. 1044

13 Dürer. *The Four Apostles*. On lime; left panel (Saint John the Evangelist and Saint Peter) 215.5 × 76 cm.; right panel (Saint Mark and Saint Paul) 214.5 × 76 cm. Signed above on the left: AD/1526. Acquired 1627 by Maximilian I from the City Council of Nuremberg. AP Nos. 545, 540

14 Hans Muelich. Born 1516 in Munich, died there 1573. *Duke Albrecht V of Bavaria*. On lime, 87 × 68 cm. Signed: H. MIELICH 1545. AP No. 4301

15 Fra Giovanni da Fiesole, called Fra Angelico. Born about 1387 in Vicchio, died in Rome 1455. *Illustration from the Legend of Saint Cosmas and Saint Damian*. On poplar, 38 × 46 cm. Three sections of the altar of S. Marco in Florence painted in 1440, have been in Munich since 1822. AP No. HG 36

16 Sandro di Mariano Filipepi, called Botticelli. Born 1444 or 1445 in Florence, died there 1510. *Lamentation.* On poplar, 140×207 cm. Probably not entirely his own work. Bought by Crown Prince Ludwig between 1814 and 1816 in Florence. AP No. 1075

17 Tiziano Vecellio, called Titian. Born about 1476/77 in Pieve di Cadore, died in Venice 1576. *The Emperor Charles V.* On canvas, 205×122 cm. Signed: Titianus F., date 1548. Probably only partly his own work. AP No. 632

18 a) Jacopo Robusti, called Tintoretto. Born 1518 in Venice, died there 1594. *Vulcan Catches Mars and Venus.* On canvas, 140×197 cm. Painted about 1545 to 1547. Acquired 1925 from the F. A. von Kaulbach collection. AP No. 9257

18 b) Nicolas Poussin. Born 1593 at Villers near Les Andelys, died in Rome 1665. *Apollo and Daphne.* On canvas, 97×131 cm. Painted between 1630 and 1635. AP No. 2334

19 Bartolomé Estéban Murillo. Born 1618 in Seville, died there 1682. *The Pastry-eaters.* On canvas, 123.6×102 cm. Painted between 1670 and 1675. Known to have been in Mannheim from 1756. AP No. 487

20 Pieter Brueghel. Born between 1525 and 1530 in Brueghel, died in Brussels 1569. *The Land of Cockayne.* On oak, 52×78 cm. Inscribed: MDLXVII BRUEGEL. Formerly in the Imperial Collection, Prague. Bought in Berlin 1917. AP No. 8940

21 Raffaelo Santi, known as Raphael. Born 1483 in Urbino, died in Rome 1520. *The Canigiani Holy Family.* On lime, 131×107 cm. Signed RAPHAEL. URBINAS. Painted about 1507, brought to Düsseldorf in 1691 as a marriage gift of Loisia de'Medici. AP No. 476

22 Gerard Ter Borch. Born 1617 in Zwolle, died in Deventer 1681. *Boy Picking Fleas from a Dog.* Canvas on oak, 35×27 cm. Inscribed: G.T.B. From the Mannheim Gallery. AP No. 589

23 Rembrandt Harmensz van Rijn. Born 1606 in Leyden, died in Amsterdam 1669. *Descent from the Cross.* On cedar, rounded at the top, 93×68 cm. Painted in 1633 at the latest for Prince Friedrich Heinrich, the Governor General of the Netherlands. Bought after 1702 for the Düsseldorf Gallery by Elector Johann Wilhelm von der Pfalz. AP No. 395

24 Peter Paul Rubens. Born 1577 in Siegen, Westphalia, died in Antwerp 1640. *The Rape of the Daughters of Leucippus.* On canvas, 222×209 cm. Painted about 1618 with the assistance of pupils. From the Düsseldorf Gallery. AP No. 321

25 Rubens. *Hélène Fourment, Wife of the Artist, with her Son Frans.* On oak, 146×102 cm. Painted about 1635, originally as a half-length picture, extra piece added later. Acquired 1698 by Max Emanuel. AP No. 315

26 Rubens. *Christ and the Penitent Sinners.* On oak, 147×130 cm. Painted about 1620. From the Düsseldorf Gallery. AP No. 329

27 Anthony van Dyck. Born 1599 in Antwerp, died in London 1641. *Rest on the Flight.* On canvas, 134×114 cm. 20 cm. at the top added later. Painted between 1627 and 1630. From Schleissheim. AP No. 555

28 a) Paul Cézanne. Born 1839 in Aix-en-Provence, died there 1906. *The Railway Cutting.* On canvas, 80×128 cm. Painted 1870/71. Anonymous presentation to the Tschudi bequest 1912. NSt. G. No. 8646

28 b) Edouard Manet. Born 1832 in Paris, died there 1883. *The Boat* (The painter Monet and his wife). On canvas, 82×100 cm. Signed: Manet. Painted 1874. Bought from an art dealer 1914. NSt. G. No. 8759

29 Manet. *Breakfast in the Studio.* On canvas, 118×145 cm. Signed: E. Manet. Presented in 1911 by Georg Ernst von Schmidt-Reissig. NSt. G. No. 8638

30 Pablo Picasso. Born 1881 in Malaga, now living near Antibes. *Madame Soler.* On canvas, 100×73 cm. Signed: Picasso. Painted 1903. Acquired 1964. NSt. G. No. 13672

31 Edgar Degas. Born 1834 in Paris, died there 1917. *Henri Rouart and his Son.* On canvas, 92×73 cm. Signed: Degas. Acquired 1965. NSt. G. No. 13681

32 Cézanne. *Self-portrait.* On canvas, 55×47 cm. Painted between 1875 and 1877. Presented in 1912 by Eduard Arnold and Robert von Mendelssohn. NSt. G. No. 8648

33 Vincent van Gogh. Born 1853 in Groot Zundert (Holland), died in Auvers-sur-Oise 1890. *View of Arles.* On canvas, 72×92 cm. Painted 1889. Anonymous gift to the Tschudi bequest 1912. NSt. G. No. 8671

34 Karl Spitzweg. Born 1808 in Munich, died there 1885. *Begging Clarinet Player.* On wood, 47×17 cm. Signed: S within the lozenge. Acquired 1917. NP No. 8944

35 Arnold Böcklin. Born 1827 in Basle, died in San Domenico near Fiesole 1901. *The Play of the Waves.* On canvas, 180×236 cm. Signed: A. Böcklin. Painted 1883. Presented by Baron Jan Wendelstadt. NP No. 7754

36 Franz von Lenbach. Born 1836 in Schrobenhausen (Upper Bavaria), died in Munich 1904. *The Shepherd Boy.* On canvas, 104×151 cm. Signed: F. Lenbach, 1860. Sch. No. 11450

37 Hans von Marées. Born 1837 in Elberfeld, died in Rome 1887. *Double Portrait of Marées and Lenbach.* On canvas, 54×62 cm. Painted 1863. Presented by W. Lindenschmit 1891. NSt. G. No. 7874

38 Wilhelm Leibl. Born 1844 in Cologne, died in Würzburg 1900. *Fräulein Lina Kirchdorffer.* On canvas, 111×83 cm. Painted 1871/72. Acquired 1907. NSt. G. No. 8446

39 Max Liebermann. Born 1847 in Berlin, died there 1935. *Old Woman with Goats.* On canvas, 127×172 cm. Signed: M. Liebermann, 90. Acquired 1891. NSt. G. No. 7815

40 Oskar Kokoschka. Born 1886 in Pöchlarn, now living in Switzerland. *Venice.* On canvas, 75×95 cm. Signed OK. Painted 1910. Acquired 1925. NSt. G. No. 9328

41 Emil Hansen, called Nolde. Born 1867 in Nolde (Kreis Tondern), died in Seebüll 1956. *The Windmill.* On canvas, 73.5×37 cm. Signed: Emil Nolde. Painted 1932. NSt. G. No. 11392

42 Giovanni Segantini. Born 1858 in Arco, died near Pontresina 1899. *Ploughing in the Engadine.* On canvas, 116×227 cm. Signed: GS 1890. Acquired 1896. NSt. G. No. 7997

COLLECTION OF GRAPHIC ART

As early as the sixteenth century Munich possessed the basis of a collection of graphic art. In his inventory of the art treasures of Duke Albrecht V from the year 1598, Johann Baptist Fickler mentions a cupboard containing books of art and amongst them collected volumes of Dürer's prints. Immediately following this, he describes a "cabinet with 74 drawers, all of which were filled with copperplate engravings and free-hand drawings, both mounted and unmounted, and a number of woodcuts". These volumes are for the most part lost. Since Fickler gives us no more than this brief description of the contents of the cabinet, it is not possible to ascertain whether or to what extent this treasure now forms part of the present collection.

The history of the State Collection of Graphic Art as we know it today really only begins in the eighteenth century in the Palatine Residence of Mannheim. Here in the late autumn of 1758 the Elector Karl Theodor commissioned the Court painter and director of the Düsseldorf Art Gallery, Lambert Krahe, to set up a collection of drawings and engravings. The foundation may have been occasioned by the general tendency of the eighteenth century towards a comprehensive extension and arrangement of the princely collections, together with the current fashion for making collections of graphic art, and not least by pedagogical interests, in particular the provision of a collection of drawings to serve as examples for the newly established Mannheim Academy of Drawing. For years before and after the foundation Karl Theodor and his agents worked to acquire sketches and prints. The inventory drawn up in 1780/81 was able to list as many as 59,439 prints, in addition to 4,936 duplicates, and 8,728 sketches.

The number of the sketches by Rembrandt is ex-pressly mentioned in this inventory. Of the 373 drawings, all of which bear the stamp of the earliest Mannheim collection (Lugt 620), most have proved after examination not to be the work of Rembrandt's own hand. Nevertheless this section is still today one of the most important features of the collection, being among the oldest complete Rembrandt groups and containing such masterly sketches by Rembrandt himself as *Saskia in Bed, Christ and the Woman Taken in Adultery, Back of a Seated Female Nude* and the preliminary sketch for the Stockholm *Conspiracy of Claudius Civilis.*

Like the rest of the collections in Mannheim, the collection of engravings was at first unaffected by the removal in 1777 of the Residence to Munich following Karl Theodor's succession to the united Bavaria-Palatinate. Only in 1794, with the Revolutionary Wars was it decided to move the art treasures to Munich.

The conclusion of the Mannheim epoch is marked by the completion between 1802 and 1804 by the inspector of the gallery, Georg Dillis, and the director of the collection, Matthias Schmidt, of a "Catalogue of the Drawings to be found in the Mannheim Collection" which contained 9,600 items. The list begins with the 556 sketches which had been framed and hung in the rooms of the Mannheim collection, including Mantegna's *Dancing Muse,* Titian's *Leaping Horseman and Fallen Warrior* and the study by Greco after Michelangelo's figure *Day.* Then follow – often wrongly attributed – apart from the Rembrandt drawings already mentioned, sketches by Michelangelo, Raphael, Fra Bartolommeo, Annibale Carracci, Rubens, Jordaens, Watteau and others. A supplement lists volumes of collected drawings including the two *Palma Giovine* volumes and three volumes of sketches by the Galli Bibiena family. In the inventory are the impressive results of some fifty years of acquisitions, to which the present collection is indebted for its first-rate sketches by earlier foreign masters. Amongst the most important of the Old-German sketches are Schongauer's *Head of an Angel* and a fragment of a *Triumphal Procession* by Hans Holbein the Younger.

In December of 1804 the collection of sketches and the collection of engravings were separated. The former came under the direction of Georg Dillis and the latter remained in the care of Matthias Schmidt. Schmidt brought the engravings from the gallery in the Court garden to his house, and from there they were moved in 1806 to the former Jesuit College; it was in this building that, in 1808, they were once again made accessible to the public for the first time since their removal from Mannheim. In 1839 the collection of engravings found a new home on the ground floor of the Old Pinakothek. In 1842, after several moves within Munich, the collection of sketches was also brought there, and in 1846 both collections were once again brought under the same administration.

Soon after they came to Munich the collections received considerable additions of prints and sketches from the secularised Bavarian monasteries (such as Prüfening, Benediktbeuern, Tegernsee). Cranach the Elder's *Saint Martin* came to Munich from Prüfening and Wolf Huber's *Battle at Pavia* probably from Benediktbeuern. 39 sketches by Claude Lorrain were bought from the Mannheim art dealer Domenico Artaria in 1804, but today most of these are no longer considered to be his work. In 1812 the Royal District Commission of Innsbruck transferred fifty drawings to Munich including many sketches by Peter Candid. In 1822 the collection received from Motzler, an antiquarian from Freising, a total of 1,161 folios. They contained principally the works of South German artists – the most important sketch was Albrecht Altdorfer's *Beheading of Saint Catherine* – and some considerable Italian drawings, such as a fine figure drawing by Pontormo. Two years later King Max I bought the estate of Baron Stephan von Stengel and so brought into the collection such drawings as Dürer's studies of fighting animals, Huber's *Fall to Death of Marcus Curtius*, the *Mountain Landscape* by Pieter Brueghel the Elder, and the draft of an altar-piece by Rosso Fiorentino.

In 1822 the direction of the collection of engravings fell to the remarkably able and competent Franz Brulliot. He began at once to draw up an inventory of the material, and to withdraw duplicates which he sold by auction in order to produce the means necessary to consolidate the collection. In 1830, during his term of office, with assistance from the king, the Baron von Aretin's collection of engravings was bought, containing a considerable number of etchings by Rembrandt and his school. Thus it was possible to enlarge the already important collection of Rembrandt's graphic art. We are particularly indebted to Brulliot for the transfer which he succeeded in arranging in 1835 of the uncaptioned woodcuts and engravings of the fifteenth century from the Court and State Library to the collection of engravings. Since that time the Munich collection has been famous throughout the world in the sphere of early German graphic art. Brulliot became an important figure in the history of the study of the graphic arts with his three-volumed *Dictionnaire des Monogrammes*.

There was a change in the policy of acquisition at about the middle of the century. Attention was turned more and more to the work of contemporary and predominantly native artists. On the other hand opportunities which would never recur, to acquire important examples of older graphic art were allowed to slip by unexploited. The purchase in 1848 of more than two and a half thousand pencil drawings and oil sketches which Johann Moritz Rugendas made in the course of his several journeys to South America between 1821 and 1847, is characteristic of the altered policy.

On his death in 1868 King Ludwig I left to the collection the so-called *King Ludwig Album* containing 20 pictures in oils and 178 water-colours and sketches, which had been presented to him by the Munich artists on the occasion of the unveiling of the great *Bavaria* statue in 1850. Amongst the remaining 2,000 sketches and engravings which the king had owned were the delightful water-colour landscapes of Georg von Dillis and Carl Rottmann, imbued with the spirit of the Mediterranean. Outstanding amongst the older masterpieces is the *Head of a Man* by Dürer, which Ludwig had acquired in 1810 on the dissolution of the Praun cabinet in Nuremberg. From the bequest of Ludwig II, the collection received its first sketches by Feuerbach and Genelli. 25

In 1884 it acquired 46 engravings of the fifteenth century, chiefly works by the Master E.S., whose work is well represented in the collection today: his alphabet of figures is to be found only here in its complete form. 1,807 landscape and architectural sketches by Leo von Klenze were presented by his children in 1885. In 1894 a legacy from Count Friedrich von Schack added 45 sketches by Feuerbach, Genelli and Schwind to the collection. A particular stroke of luck in 1889 was the addition of 2,500 sketches mainly by Bavarian artists of the sixteenth to eighteenth centuries, presented by the Reichsrat Hugo Ritter von Maffei. These folios had previously belonged to the art dealer Felix Halm and had been unsuccessfully offered for sale to the collection by his widow in 1811.

In 1831 Franz Brulliot wrote that the collection of engravings had a considerable influence, not only on art studies but also on all sorts of crafts. His words reflect the view held throughout almost the whole of the nineteenth century of the purpose of such a collection. In 1854 engravings were even lent out to the Nymphenburg porcelain factory. Meanwhile art historians brought about a new appreciation of the collection for its distinction, its originality, in short for the fine quality of its individual items. At the head of this new era stands Wilhelm Schmidt, director of the collection from 1885 to 1904. We are indebted to him for the first published selection of free-hand sketches from the collection.

Since much that was in the collection of engravings at that time no longer satisfied the higher standards demanded in the quality of the printing and the state of preservation, Otto Weigmann, in the twenties, sought to remedy this, particularly in the sphere of German sixteenth-century engraving and the Rembrandt section. In 1920 the collection received the gift of Dürer's *Life of the Virgin* in exceptionally fine prints, which had been produced before the publication in book form in 1511.

Acquisitions since 1900 have mainly been further additions to those sections where the strength of the collection already lay. In 1915 further drawings by Carl Rottmann were added to the collection, and also sketches by Peter Cornelius from whose estate a further 100 drawings were acquired in 1963. The number of sketches by Schwind increased to a total of 359. In 1908 Count Moy presented 120 drawings by Wilhelm Busch, and in 1913 Hugo Reisinger

made a gift of 40 particularly fine sketches by Marées. Amongst the contemporary artists who had work accepted were Käthe Kollwitz in 1908, Edvard Munch in 1912, and in 1918 Max Beckmann, Erich Heckel, Paul Klee, Oskar Kokoschka, Wilhelm Lehmbruck and Emil Nolde.

The time after 1933 brought irreparable losses to the Collection of Graphic Art. Part of the already rather small section of modern graphic art fell victim to the "degenerate art" campaign, while in 1944 almost a third of the total contents were destroyed during a fire at the New Pinakothek where the collection had been housed since 1917. It included a large part of the French and the whole of the collection of English engravings. In addition the very extensive art library was destroyed.

After the end of the war, in spite of great difficulties, a start was made on the arduous task of rebuilding the Collection of Graphic Art, at first in the premises of the Bavarian National Museum and, from 1949, in the house at No. 10 Meiserstrasse. There is thus all the more reason to feel gratified with the success so far achieved! As a basis for the sections which were to be built up again, the Bavarian National Museum transferred 6,000 landscape sketches and 20,000 portrait engravings and portrait lithographs. The number of old masters was increased by the addition of sketches by Amberger, Burgkmair the Elder, S. Beham, Lautensack, Rottenhammer, I. Günther, Veronese, J. Bassano, Pietro da Cortona, D. Fetti, Watteau and others. Romantic art was represented in the collection by the addition of the sketch books of F. Horny and Catel, and the drawings by F. Olivier, Wasmann, J. A. Koch, Schwind, Blechen and not least by C. D. Friedrich. Drawings by artists such as Beckmann, Dix, Heckel, Kirchner, Mueller and Schmidt-Rottluff as well as engravings by these artists, give us once again an impression of German graphic art in the first decades of this century. French engraving of the eighteenth and nineteenth centuries is also well represented once again; a uniquely fine specimen of Toulouse-Lautrec's complete *Elles* series, which came from the archives of Gustave Pellet, the printer of *Elles*, stands out as the most important acquisition. The leading contemporary Italian and French artists are represented by at least one example of each, and Picasso indeed by quite a number. A start was made to repair the losses in English engravings helped by a gift of 89 Hogarth etchings. In recent years two

26

large bequests have immeasurably enriched the collection. In 1958 in memory of her husband Ludwig W. Gutbier, Ella Gutbier bequeathed 634 examples of German engravings of the nineteenth and twentieth centuries, in which the most important items are those of Expressionism. In 1964 the Max Kade Foundation of New York presented to the Society of Friends of the Collection of Graphic Art in Munich 57 masterpieces of graphic art of outstanding quality. Amongst the 28 etchings by Rembrandt there is for example the *Hundred Guilder Print* in one of the rare examples on India paper. Besides Rembrandt the works of Schongauer, Dürer and Lucas van Leyden represent further major items in the Kade bequest, whose brilliance outshine the other legacies to the Collection of Graphic Art in this century.

DESCRIPTION OF ILLUSTRATIONS

45 Tegernsee Monastery (?). *Christ on the Cross with the Tegernsee Coat of Arms.* Woodcut (coat of arms printed with a separate wood impress). Illuminated, 410×270 mm. (Schreiber 932). About 1420/40. Acquired 1835. Inv. No. 118120

46 Albrecht Dürer. Born 1471 in Nuremberg, died there 1528. *The Rejection of the Sacrifice of Joachim.* Woodcut, 291×209 mm. (Bartsch 77). About 1502/03. Page from sample prints of the "Life of the Virgin" which appeared before the edition in book form in 1511. Presented 1920. Inv. No. 1920:133

47 Wolf Huber. Born about 1485 in Feldkirch in Vorarlberg, died in Passau 1553. *Mountainous Landscape with Wooden Bridge.* Pen in brown, 211×160 mm. 1515. Acquired 1891. Inv. No. 33434

48 Michelangelo Buonarroti. Born 1475 in Caprese in Casentino, died in Rome 1564. *Saint Peter.* Pen in brown inks, preliminary sketching in red chalk. Background coloured in light blue at later date, 317×195 mm. (Dussler 186). About 1488/95. Copy of the figure of Peter in the "Tribute Money" fresco by Masaccio (Florence, Cappella Brancacci). The studies of the arm sketched on the picture in red chalk are probably his own work. From the Mannheim collection. Inv. No. 2191

49 Tiziano Vecellio, called Titian. Born about 1476/77 in Pieve di Cadore, died in Venice 1576. *Leaping Horseman and Fallen Warrior.* Black and white chalk on yellowed blue paper, marked in squares in black, 348×247 mm. From the Mannheim collection. Inv. No. 2981

50 a) Rembrandt Harmensz van Rijn. Born 1606 in Leyden, died in Amsterdam 1669. *Christ and the Woman Taken in Adultery.* Pen drawing in brown; brown, grey, pink and red wash, 170×202 mm. (Benesch 1074). About 1659/60. The writing on the lower edge in Rembrandt's own hand can be translated thus: "One of the scribes, seeking to entangle Christ in his talk, would not await an answer." From the Mannheim collection. Inv. No. 1421

50 b) Claude Lorrain, properly Claude Gellée. Born 1600 in the castle of Chamagne near Mirecourt, died in Rome 1682. *Landscape.* Chalk, pen and brush in bistre, 257×389 mm. Transferred from the estate of King Ludwig I 1868. Inv. No. 21081

51 Rembrandt. *The Proclamation to the Shepherds.* Etching, 261×218 mm. (Münz 199 III). 1634. Presented by the Max Kade Foundation to the Society of Friends of the Collection of Graphic Art 1964. Inv. No. 1964:455D

52 Carl Rottmann. Born 1797 in Handschuhsheim near Heidelberg, died in Munich 1850. *Santorin.* Water-colour over preliminary sketching in pencil, 281×382 mm. 1835. Acquired from the estate of King Ludwig I in 1868. Preliminary study for a mural in the Greek series in the New Pinakothek which was never realised. Inv. No. 21394

53 Hans von Marées. Born 1837 in Elberfeld, died in Rome 1887. *Two-horse Team.* Red chalk, 380×405 mm. About 1880. Presented 1913. Inv. No. 1913:44

54 a) Franz Marc. Born 1880 in Munich, died in Verdun 1916. *Conflict.* Pencil, 97×160 mm. 1915. Page No. 24 in the Sketch-book from Active Service. Acquired 1955. Inv. No. 1955:57Z

54 b) Marc. *Bird.* Pencil, 97×160 mm. 1915. Page No. 32 in his Sketch-book from Active Service. Acquired 1955. Inv. No. 1955:64Z

55 Pablo Picasso. Born 1881 in Malaga, now living near Antibes. *Minotaur bending over Sleeping Girl.* Dry point, 296×366 mm. (Suite Vollard No. 93). 1933 (Boisgeloup 18 juin XXXIII). Acquired 1960. Inv. No. 1960:518D

56 Henri de Toulouse-Lautrec. Born 1864 in Albi, died in Malcomé 1901. *La Clownesse assise* (Mlle. Cha-U-Kao). Colour lithograph, 520×400 mm. (Delteil 180). Page from the "Elles" series. Acquired 1962. Inv. No. 1962:394D

BAVARIAN NATIONAL MUSEUM

The Bavarian National Museum was founded by King Maximilian II in the middle of the nineteenth century. The intention of the king was to bring about a general appreciation of the high values and achievements of the past. The museum was to encourage the contacts and mutual obligations between the rulers and the people, and make clear the great continuity of historical growth, in order to bring before the citizens of his State the far-reaching importance of the monuments and documents handed down to them from the past.

The founding of the museum was preceded by the publication of the book *The Antiquities and Works of Art of the Bavarian Ruling House* which had been written at the instigation of King Maximilian. The historical part of this publication was entrusted to the director of the Private House and State Archives, K. M. Freiherr von Aretin, and the artistic part to J. H. von Hefner-Alteneck. In 1853 Aretin submitted to the king the plan for the establishment of a "Wittelsbach Museum", which would bring together the treasures of the ruling house "in originals and reproductions". The plan for the museum was the direct result of the central idea expressed in Aretin's book. But Maximilian also wished "that notice should be drawn to everything that was particular to the Bavarian people and notable in the history of the country, so that the collection should be a truly national collection, similar to the French one in the Palace of Versailles". A plan on a grand scale, to put on display those forces which had influenced the course of history. In 1855 the king decided that the name of the collection should be the "Bavarian National Museum". This was directly connected with the accepted French idea of the *Musée National*. Aretin was able to take over a number of objects from the Munich Residence and the royal palaces to which belonged earlier Wittelsbach art collections. In this way the National Museum dates back to those *Kunstkammern* which had come into being under the Renaissance and Humanism of the late sixteenth century. In the first inventory which Duke Maximilian I ordered his lawyer Johann Fickler to draw up in 1598, objects are mentioned which even today rank among the treasures of the Bavarian National Museum.

The first place in which the notable objects from all parts of the country were brought together was the *Herzog Max Burg*. In 1859 a monumental new building was erected for use as a museum on the Maximiliansstrasse where it widens into a sort of forum, directly opposite the building of the Bavarian State Government. This stressed yet again the importance that was attached to the cultural rôle of this museum. An historical gallery was planned for the first floor of the three-storied central part of the building. This was at the special wish of the king who had been remarkably impressed by the historical gallery at Versailles. In it, over a hundred paintings were to proclaim the deeds of glory in the history of Bavaria. The museum was opened in 1867. Aretin's arrangement of the exhibits attached less importance to the significance of individual objects; he was much more concerned with the impression made by the rooms as historical illustrations. For this purpose he used set pieces made up of the furnishings from old churches, castles and patrician houses.

After Aretin's death in 1868, J. H. von Hefner-Alteneck became director of this museum as well as general curator of art treasures and antiquities in Bavaria. Influenced by the contemporary revival of the decorative arts, he saw the duty and aim of the museum principally in its development as a school for artists and craftsmen. After the example of the South Kensington Museum in London and the newly founded museums of decorative art in Vienna and Berlin, Hefner-Alteneck gathered a collection of designs for contemporary industrial arts. The technical collection, grouped according to material, was intended to provide a basis for the development of aesthetic appreciation.

Both these considerations, the plan of Aretin to illustrate the history of civilisation and Hefner-Alteneck's programme for instruction in applied art, were taken into account in the two-storied building which had been erected at the turn of the century on the Prinzregentenstrasse by Gabriel von Seidl. The exterior of this building has the character of a generously laid out castle in Renaissance style. The central portion crowned by a high tower, faces onto the street, and contains the entrance hall. The upper story houses the administrative rooms and the library. The collections are arranged in the wings of the building which enclose courtyards.

Originally these courtyards were used to show works of art illustrating the history of civilisation, but this was changed after the destruction suffered in the last war. But still standing unchanged to this day in the southern west court is the monumental fountain group *Mars and Venus with Amor*, which came from the Kirchheim castle near Mindelheim, an outstanding work of art of late Florentine Renaissance character, created by the Netherlandish sculptor Hubert Gerhard in 1584 for Count Hans Fugger.

The arrangement of the buildings takes into account the museum's programme. The collections relating to the history of art and of civilisation are set out in historical sequence on the ground floor. In this way the visitor is able to walk through the various periods of history. In the upper story, grouped according to material, are the exhibits of applied art. In addition, on the ground floor of the west wing there is the section on folklore and folk art, and on the ground floor of the east wing, the display of crèches.

Within the traditional sphere of the museum there are also the State's Prehistoric Collection, temporarily housed in a side building erected in 1936, and in another nearby building the "New Collection" as it is called, a museum founded in 1926 for modern applied art, and finally the Museum of the Bavarian Army, which is soon to be transferred to the Ducal palace of Ingolstadt.

During the Second World War these museums were badly damaged by bombing. In rebuilding, the aim has been to recreate the bold design of Gabriel von Seidl. The new arrangements sought to achieve, within the limits set by the rooms, a greater emphasis on individual works and groups of works, rather than the more general impressions which the original layout had aimed to produce.

The first room had originally housed the prehistoric and Roman-provincial exhibits, which now form part of the State's Prehistoric Collection. This room is now devoted to the art of the early and high Middle Ages. Amongst the earliest and most important exhibits are the ornaments worked in precious metal with almandine inlays from the second half of the seventh century, which were found in a tomb in Wittislingen near Lauingen. In addition there are famous examples of early ivory carving, including the early Christian panel with the representation of Christ's Ascension, the fragments of an altar antependium of Emperor Otto I from Magdeburg Cathedral, and masterpieces in the Romanesque style. The tradition of the representation of the occult is illustrated in exhibits ranging from the so-called casket of Kunigunde from Bamberg, carved in walrus tusk in about the year 1,000, to the lion's head decoration on a ceremonial chair of the twelfth century. There are also valuable enamels, liturgical instruments cast in bronze, reliquaries and candle holders, as well as works of art imported from distant countries. Among the latter are the Willigis chasuble in Byzantine silk from Aschaffenburg or Mainz, a Syrian glass goblet from Aleppo or the English needlework on a mitre from Seligenthal monastery near Landshut. These works of minor art contrast with the monumental stone sculptures, which reflect the energy of the medieval masons – fine examples are the statue of Christ giving blessing from the Reichenbach monastery in the Upper Palatinate, and the sculptures from the Wessobrunn monastery of the middle of the thirteenth century. Wood sculpture, equally lapidary in style, is represented by splendid figures of Christ and the Virgin, some still showing the original coating.

A particularly impressive work is a majestic figure of the Virgin from Regensburg, whose attitude of deep absorption is typical of early Gothic style. The beautiful stone figure of the *Madonna of the Rose Bush* from Straubing and the gentle piety of a carved group with Christ and Saint John, probably made for a

29

convent on the Upper Rhine or in Upper Swabia, are evidence of the enhanced poetic feeling in the mysticism of the fourteenth century.

About 1400 a new awareness of the human element in art emerges. This gradual development can be seen in the third room of the museum in a series of mainly Franconian tombstones of knights.

In the fourth room are early examples of large-scale panel-painting: the wonderfully tender and ethereal paintings from the Munich Church of St. Augustine, and the paintings of the Passion which even as early as this seem almost naturalistic, in the winged altar of 1429 from the Bamberg Church of the Franciscans. Many influences from Bohemia are obvious in the art of South Germany at this time. An important centre of artistic talent had grown up there, particularly at the time of Karl IV. Probably also of Bohemian origin is the winged altar from the Pähl castle near Weilheim, outstanding in the harmony of its colours and also in the rare quality of preservation of the original appearance. The addition of contemporary masterpieces of sculpture show it off to its best advantage. The vespers picture carved in stone from the Seeon monastery in the Chiemgau has a unique fervour. A carved seated figure of the Holy Virgin which still retains in its coating and gilding the inspiring luminosity of the early fifteenth century, is from the same monastery.

The museum also houses fine examples from the wide sphere of sacred and secular crafts of late Gothic times, including a small canopied altar from Cologne which heralds that harmony of carpentry, sculpture and painting which was to be the essence of the late Gothic altar.

In the "Tegernsee Hall" there is the enthroned figure of the Holy Virgin from Brixen, in a fine state of preservation. It is an early work of the wood-carver and painter from Ulm, Hans Multscher, whose work is further represented in the museum by the delicate figure of a winged angel in flight from his famous *Sterzing Altar* (1456 to 1458). The model, carved in 1435 in Solnhofen stone by Hans Multscher on order of Duke Ludwig the Bearded, for his marble tombstone in the Church of St. Mary (*Liebfrauenkirche*) in Ingolstadt, which was never carried out, has unique significance both as an artistic and at the same time historical document. To the same period belongs the splendid wooden figure of the Holy Virgin from the altar which Jakob Kaschauer completed in 1443

in Vienna for the Freising Cathedral. At her feet is the small kneeling figure of the founder, Bishop Nikodemus della Scala (the Scaligers were, as the Bavarians put it, the lords "of the ladder"), and the beginning of the new era can be seen in the combination of the monumental nature of the statue of the Virgin and the naturalistic portrayal of the founder.

The adjoining rooms contain original domestic interiors, which by reminding us of the character of the buildings from which these interiors were taken, provide us with a lively illustration of the social structure in Upper Germany in late Gothic times. Particularly noteworthy are the office of the Augsburg weavers' house decorated with a series of illustrations, a wooden ceiling and door frames from the bishop's palace at Oberhaus near Passau of about 1490, a wooden beamed ceiling from the bishop's palace at Füssen, a carved ceiling from the former House of the Teutonic Knights in Nuremberg, and a fresco depicting the ancestors of the House of Wittelsbach from the *Alter Hof*, the earliest Residence in Munich. When we consider moreover that Gabriel von Seidl arranged the next large hall on the basis of motifs from the Augsburg Cathedral cloister, it becomes clear that this sequence of rooms is a unique reflection of the *potestas* of the later Middle Ages.

Splendid examples of late Gothic applied art are displayed within these rooms: imposing furniture, tapestries in which the colours have a wonderful luminosity, glass-paintings (such as those from the Munich Church of St. Mary), wooden sculptures and painted panels from winged altars. Particularly noteworthy is the carved devotional rendering of an angel leading the Christ Child as if to dance, from the convent of the Ursulines in Landsberg-on-the-Lech, as well as an Annunciation group in alabaster from Würzburg, dating from 1484.

In the arrangement of the sculptures and paintings the intention has been to express the specifically native characteristics, particularly by bringing together works of early Bavarian and Austrian masters in the "Great Church Hall". Here were displayed the uncompromising carvings of Erasmus Grasser (Munich), the ecstatic intensity of expression in the painting of Jan Pollack, the absolute mastery of form of Michael Pacher (Bruneck) and the gentle radiance in the altar-pieces of Hans Klocker (Brixen). To these we must add the paintings on glass of the late fourteenth century from the Church of the Minorites in Regensburg.

At the end of the fifteenth century the personalities of individual artists stand out more clearly than before. It was the age of the young Albrecht Dürer, while in Nuremberg there was the disturbingly forceful Veit Stoss, in Augsburg, Michael Erhart and his son Gregor, sculptor to Emperor Maximilian – his artistic skill is demonstrated in the Bavarian National Museum by a figure of the Virgin in a proud upright posture. In Würzburg there was Tilman Riemenschneider. His work is outstandingly well represented in the National Museum by the *Mary Magdalene with Six Angels*, from the Münnerstadt high altar (1490 to 1492), a relief from a wing of the same altar, a painted figure of *Saint Sebastian*, the altar from Gerolzhofen, and by the figures which, as is characteristic of Riemenschneider, were not intended to be finished with a coating of colour, and for this reason show a particular refinement in the finish given to the surface.

South German art of the late Gothic period closes with the Danube style. The works of Leinberger, which are represented in great number in the National Museum, combine late Gothic expressionism with an emotion that already foreshadows the Baroque. It is typical of the breadth of his skill that the monumental wooden figure of *Saint James* still belongs to the traditional altar sculpture, while his *Calvary* relief of 1516 is an expressive example of that small-scale sculpture of the German early Renaissance, which grew to such far-reaching importance.

Within the "Dachau Hall" is a most effective collection of examples of this dialogue between tradition and new development: the powerful bronze figure of the *Man Breaking a Bough* of Peter Vischer the Elder of Nuremberg, and the group carved in hard-wood of a *Burial of Christ* (1496) by the master Konrad Meit of Worms, who later achieved great fame at the court of the Archduchess Margarethe of Austria in Mechelen. The signed alabaster statuette of a *Judith* is also his work. Masterpieces by Loy Hering, Hans Daucher, Sebastian Loscher, Hans Schwarz, Hans Kels, Friedrich Hagenauer, as well as Ludwig Krug and Peter Flötner, represent fine examples of the flowering of the early Renaissance in Augsburg and Nuremberg. The large bronze group of *Martin* from Neuburg is an outstanding work of the Vischer foundry in Nuremberg. Portraits of the princes by the Court painters Hans Wertinger in Landshut and Peter Gärtner in Neuburg, and gobelins from Brussels from about 1540 all contribute to make the past live again. Many of these works had originally been commissioned by the princes in their passion for collecting treasures of art.

In the next room the combination of the coffer-work ceiling from Mantua (about 1525) with the Italian works of art of the same period, is particularly pleasing: they include bronzes by Tullio Lombardi (Venice) and Riccio (Padua), a signed stone figure by Alessandro Vittoria and a bridal chest from Mantua which belonged to the Duchess Jakobäa Maria from the Trausnitz castle; all are works of art which show how close the links were between the courts of Bavaria and Italy especially at this time.

This is also shown by the fine craft work of the plate armour in the two halls of weapons of the museum. The first hall is an enlarged copy of a hall built about 1290 within the house of the Regensburg family of the Dollingers, which was destroyed in the nineteenth century. Lances, halberds and pikes, broadswords and spears, hunting weapons and muskets are assembled here amongst armour, coats of mail and swords, to form a veritable armoury. In the second hall of weapons the etched and gilded Milan plate armour of the Salzburg Archbishop Wolf Dieter von Raitenau (1587 to 1612) is particularly worthy of note. In the nearby ordnance yard huge cannons-royal illustrate the masterly skill of German bronze casting during the Renaissance.

In the years around 1600 Italy once again exerted a decisive influence on the artistic development of Southern Germany. The new style was initiated principally by Giovanni da Bologna, a sculptor working in Florence who had been born in Northern France. His work is represented in the National Museum by six bronze reliefs depicting the Passion and also by a group in bronze.

As a result of the contacts with the Italian art of the late Renaissance and of Mannerism there grew up in the South German art of the time about 1600 a new dynamism also released by the Counter-Reformation's search for a new and more forceful imagery. Examples of this in the National Museum are the many representative works of Hans Krumper, the "Superintendent of Art" to Duke Wilhelm V, as well as those of the Court sculptor Christoph

Angermaier, who was born in Weilheim, those of the great Augsburg artist Georg Petel, who died in 1633, or those of the Zürn brothers who lived in Swabia. In addition to Florence, Antwerp, the residence of Peter Paul Rubens, also developed at this time into a focal point for European art. There is evidence of this in the collections, particularly in the carved statuette of a negress.

In addition there are exhibits which illustrate social history, such as the very fine clothes and the brilliant jewellery from the vault of the princes in Lauingen, the burial place of the Palatinate-Neuburg line of the House of Wittelsbach at the end of the sixteenth century.

In 1623 Duke Maximilian I became Elector, and court art rose to new heights. Splendid examples of this are the display cases and coin cabinets made by Augsburg and Munich craftsmen for the Elector. Their decorations allude to the love of art of the prince. The secret compartments hidden within these cabinets, opening only to the initiated, afford just those delightful surprises which are the very essence of the *Kunst- und Wunderkammern* which flourished at this time.

Valuable bowls in agate and amethyst, cups and goblets carved in rock-crystal and ivory represent some of the ceremonial vessels made in the court workshops. Such vessels were to be found in the Residence, in the luxurious apartments of the Electress Henriette Adelaide, wife of Ferdinand Maria. For the last time Italian artists were brought to the Court in Munich to build for them the Theatine Church of St. Cajetan and the central section of the Nymphenburg palace. The ceiling with the sumptuous gilded stucco decoration surrounding ceiling paintings of mythological themes came from the apartments of the Electress.

The refinement of the time in the use of all materials can even be seen in the viola da gamba which was made by Joachim Tielcke in Hamburg in 1691 for the Elector Johann Wilhelm of the Palatine branch of the House of Wittelsbach. This instrument with its inlays of tortoise-shell, ivory, mother-of-pearl and silver is the finest and most ornate exhibit the National Museum has in its collection of musical instruments. The collection is not yet restored to public exhibition.

In the unique astronomical clocks from Augsburg and Munich chronographic and astronomical infor-

mation is combined with a list of the saints in the Christian calendar. For the work on the clock casings the watchmaker had to turn to other crafts and call in moulders, case-makers, enchasers, enamellers and engravers. These clocks, enhanced by mechanically moving figures and music, demonstrate in a light-hearted manner the importance of mechanics and the pleasure taken at this time in mechanical contrivances, with which, almost by chance, technical development begins.

The boulle secretaires, coin cabinets and writing desks illustrate the splendour of the princely household of the Elector Max Emanuel, which at this time was influenced by the political and cultural supremacy of France. Max Emanuel engaged eminent artists such as Effner, de Groff and Zuccalli to come to Munich where they played an important part in the development of Bavarian Rococo. His furniture, influenced by Paris, surpasses all earlier styles in splendour of form and variety of material. We are reminded of the Elector's victories in war and of his storming of Belgrade by the Turkish trophies. His apotheosis – a rider leaping over the Fury of war, being adorned with a wreath by a goddess of victory – was the work of Wilhelm de Groff, who was trained in the service of Louis XIV.

Two completely furnished rooms, their original form unaltered in every respect, allow the visitor to experience the atmosphere of the rooms of the eighteenth century. One of middle-class elegance which came from the Moserbräu in Landshut, was used by the Bavarian ducal family; the other was the private cabinet of the Tattenbach Palace in Munich; in its architectural design it dates back to François de Cuvilliés the Younger.

Bavarian art of the eighteenth century is probably best represented here by some garden statues in sandstone, the work of the Bamberg master Ferdinand Dietz, or by wood-carvings by the Munich artist Ignaz Günther. His house madonnas and angels, in their tender charm, recall the magic of the Rococo churches of Bavaria; the figure of *Bellona*, on the other hand, dates from the end of his artistic activity which was influenced by the Viennese Academy, and shows the first traces of the cool reserve of the new Classicism.

In the magnificent, glowing church interiors of this time in Southern Germany, fresco was an essential factor in the ultimate blending of the arts. The exhibition of this flowering of art in South Germany is rounded off by a collection of oil sketches and cartoons for frescoes which sometimes show a personal originality and a degree of imagination more clearly than the frescoes themselves, which were to a large extent the joint work of a studio. The museum is indebted to the patronage of Wilhelm Reuschel of Munich for this special collection (at the moment housed in the east wing of the upper story).

The last stages of this journey through the social history of Bavaria show the contributions made to the cause of art by King Maximilian I, Ludwig I and Maximilian II, the founder of the museum. Of particular interest are the costumes of the Royal Family, including the national costume of the Greek King Otto.

In the last room there is a collection of models of the Bavarian ducal towns of Straubing, Landshut, Munich, Ingolstadt and Burghausen, built up by Jakob Sandtner in Straubing between 1568 and 1574, as well as the scale model of the Capital of Munich, which had been carried out on order of the king between 1846 and 1868; it is an illustration of a process of growth which summarises the whole of its history.

We can pick out for mention only a few especially important sections in the collections of decorative and applied art in the upper story of the building. The principal aim of the exhibition is to draw attention to the importance and individuality of the particular works of art in Bavaria and Southern Germany and at the same time to display related contemporary products, particularly in those instances where these have influenced the creation and development of the works of art in Bavaria and Southern Germany. In this way it is a kind of arts-and-crafts museum chiefly based on the outstanding products from Bavaria and Southern Germany.

The largest room in the west wing of the upper story is occupied by the ceramic collections, particularly by an extensive display of the history of porcelain. This starts out with the Meissen factory founded by August the Strong and the similar establishments which followed – of these, that of Du Paquier in Vienna was of outstanding merit – and culminates in the splendid work of the Munich factory which Count Sigmund von Haimhausen built in the small castle of Neudeck in 1753, and which since its transfer to Nymphenburg in 1761, has attained world-

wide fame, especially through the work of Franz Anton Bustelli. The magic of Nymphenburg porcelain can be appreciated more strongly here perhaps than in any other place. At the same time the contemporary products of other South German factories are extremely well represented.

The same thing is true of the museum's particularly extensive collection of faience. It owes many of the works to the bequest of the well-known connoisseur and collector Dr. Paul Heiland of Potsdam who died in 1933. Here we have a significant picture of the factories with branches throughout the whole of Central Europe, and at their midst, the Bavarian centres of production, Bayreuth, Künersberg, Schrezheim, Göggingen. The collection illustrates effectively how fundamentally the nature of faience differs from that of porcelain.

In the midst of the ceramic collections there is the "Bayreuth Hall", containing built-in panelling made by the Spindler brothers, who later worked for Friedrich II in Berlin. It came from the castle *Fantasie* near Bayreuth, together with choice examples of the ceramic art of Bayreuth, an elegant stove from the Seehof castle near Bamberg and the notable bust of Diderot made by Houdon in 1780.

These ceramic products are typical of the mercantilism of the seventeenth and eighteenth centuries. They were preceded by the fine craftsmanship of the *Hafner* ceramic work, which is shown in other rooms of this upper story in the company of brilliant exhibits in Italian majolica from the same period.

The exhibition of the goldsmith's work from the sixteenth to the eighteenth centuries presents us with yet another aspect of art. The leading centres in Germany were Augsburg and Nuremberg. In the sacred and secular objects of the collection we can see the artistic skill of these craftsmen, who in the various techniques they used in the working of precious metals – casting, raising, chasing and embossing – were able to create over and over again new results in the service of aristocratic elegance or middle-class affluence.

Nearby there is a unique collection of plaques. The relief illustrations on these plaques have all the refinement of graphic art. They represent brilliantly the life work of Peter Flötner in Nuremberg. We can also see splendid examples of the work of Jamnitzer and of the Augsburg craftsman Wallbaum. Once again works from the Netherlands, France and Italy are 33 evidence of the parallel developments in art and craftsmanship.

In the east wing of the upper story is the "Hall of Honour", which until the re-establishment of the Museum of the Bavarian Army in Ingolstadt, continues to house the complete range of the standards of the former Bavarian Army. In another room there are the official robes of the courtly society of the House of Wittelsbach, that is, the Order of the Knights of Saint George and Saint Hubert.

We then come to the built-in panelling by Franz Xaver Schwanthaler from the former Cotta Palace in Munich, used once again for the purpose of re-creating the atmosphere of the original interior. Two rooms displaying costumes and fashionable accessories of the eighteenth and early nineteenth centuries are reminders of the enchanting elegance in the carefree society of the *ancien régime* and another example of French influences.

On the ground floor of the east wing we find the world-renowned collection of Nativity cribs, which we owe to a great extent to the flair and zeal for collecting of the Councillor of Commerce Max Schmederer and his bequest of 1892. In more than forty groupings built up like stage settings, scenes from the birth and life of Christ are presented in their relation to the Church Year. They are masterpieces of minor plastic art of the eighteenth and early nine-

teenth centuries from Bavaria, Austria, Italy and France, which bear witness to a powerful religious imagination. It should be stressed here that this crib art has its origins in the imagery of mysticism.

Corresponding to this exhibition is the section devoted to folklore and folk art on the ground floor of the west wing, starting with reconstructions of old rooms from peasant houses which illustrate the variety of form and colour in the household furnishings in the South German countryside. In addition there are splendid examples of popular wood-carving and ceramic art, as well as national costumes and fine specimens of textile weaving, in every case chosen for their typically local characteristics.

A strange world is opened up to us in the collection of works of popular religious faith gathered together and presented to the museum by Professor Dr. Kriss. Starting with works from the Greek islands we are shown in a unique way how, right up to the present day, religious conceptions are bound to nature. Particularly in examples from Bavaria and the Alps, the popular view of the story of the life and sufferings of Christ is systematically demonstrated, with all the magic and superstition which surround it.

And so the circle of the exhibits is complete: in this museum the art is just as much universal as, in the words of its founder, it is "characteristic of the people".

DESCRIPTION OF ILLUSTRATIONS

59 1. *Hooped Clasp*. Cast in silver, gilded. Cloisonné with almandines and molten green glass. Niello with filigree decoration. Probably made in the Rhineland about the middle of the 7th century. On the reverse an inscription in capital letters worked in niello recalls in the manner of ancient burial inscriptions, the memory of Uffila, and praises her Christian virtues. Found in Wittislingen. Inv. No. Cat. IV, 1891

2. *Disc-shaped Clasp*. Chased gold-foil. Cloisonné, inlaid with almandines, and filigree ornamentation. Alemannic work from the middle of the 7th century. Found in a common burial place in Wittislingen (Kreis Lauingen, on the Danube). Inv. No. Cat. IV, 1905

60 *The Maries at the Sepulchre and Christ's Ascension into Heaven*. Ivory. Height 18.7 cm., width 11.6 cm. Italian, about 400. Acquired 1860 as part of the collection of Martin von Reider from Bamberg. Inv. No. Ma 157

61 *Crucifix*. In lime, coating lost. Height 65 cm., width 57 cm. Supposedly from the Church of St. George in Milbertshofen. Between 1100 and 1120. Inv. No. 30/2059

62 *The Pähl Altar*. Centre panel: the Crucifixion. Tempera painting with a gold ground on wooden panel. Height 103 cm., width 68 cm. About 1400. From the Pähl castle near Weilheim (Upper Bavaria). Inv. No. Ma 2377

63 *Holy Virgin with the Rose Bush*. Green sandstone with original coating. Height 134 cm. From Straubing. Between 1320 and 1330. Inv. No. 16/287

64 *Cradle of the Christ Child*. Painted wooden box. Cradle: length 27 cm., height 13 cm.; stand: length 32 cm. South Germany, about 1320. Inv. No. Ma 2399

65 *Unicorn Hunt*. Fragment of a back cloth. Worked in wool. Height 74 cm., width 150 cm. Franconia (Nuremberg?), about 1450/60. Inv. No. T. 1690

66 *Group, Christ with Saint John*. Oak. Height 67.5 cm., width 44 cm., depth 28.5 cm. Upper Rhine – Lake Constance, about 1320. Bequest of Dr. Franz Haniel, Munich, 1965. Inv. No. 65/38

67 *Mary with the Child Jesus*. Lime with original coating. Height 108 cm. Comes from the Benedictine monastery of Seeon near Traunstein. About 1425. Inv. No. Ma 1126

68 Hans Multscher. Born about 1400 in Reichenhofen (Allgäu), died in Ulm 1467. *Model for the Burial Stone of Duke Ludwig the Bearded of Bavaria-Ingolstadt.* In Solnhofen stone. Height 58 cm., width 31 cm. Ulm, 1435. Inv. No. Ma 936

69 Hans Leinberger, active from 1513 to about 1530 in Landshut. *Saint James the Elder.* Lime with slight remains of the original coating. Back is hollowed out. Height 195 cm. About 1525. Inv. No. 15/114

70 Tilman Riemenschneider. Born about 1460 in Heiligenstadt, died in Würzburg 1531. *Saint John.* Lime (worked in the round), uncoated. Height 56 cm. From the Chapel of St. Mary in Würzburg. Between 1505 and 1510. Acquired 1858 as part of the Martinengo collection. Inv. No. Ma 1330

71 Riemenschneider. *Mary Magdalene with Six Angels.* Lime, uncoated. Height 187 cm. From the shrine of the Münnerstadt high altar. About 1490/92. Acquired 1901. Inv. No. Ma 4094

72 *The Infant Jesus with Angel.* In lime (worked in the round), with original coating. Height 74 cm. From the Convent of the Ursulines, Landsberg/Lech, about 1480. Hair of the Child Jesus cut away, probably in Baroque times, to enable a wig to be fitted. Inv. No. 20/268

73 Peter Vischer the Elder. Born about 1460 in Nuremberg, died there 1529. *Kneeling Man* ("Man Breaking a Bough"). In bronze, solid casting from wax model. Height 36.8 cm. The date 1490 is cast in base. Inv. No. Ma 1983

74 Georg Petel. Born about 1590 in Weilheim, died in Augsburg about 1633. *Saint Sebastian.* Ivory statuette, worked in the round. Height 29.6 cm. About 1628/29. Signed IPF in the hollow of the branch against the right shoulder. Inv. No. R 4600

75 Jakob Sandtner. *Model of Munich* (detail). In lime, scale 1:750. Made in Straubing in 1572 for Albrecht V of Bavaria. Inv. No. 10 I 16

76 *Toy Model of Jouster.* Wooden toy of horse and rider with plate armour and dressed in silk. Height 42 cm. Nuremberg, about 1530. Painting on the horse cover and the helmet crest indicate that this knightly toy once belonged to the patrician family of Holzschuher in Nuremberg. Inv. No. W 940 and W 942

77 Franz Anton Bustelli. Born 1723 in Locarno, died in Nymphenburg 1763. *The Sleeper Disturbed.* Porcelain, painted. Height 22 cm. Nymphenburg, produced 1755 to 1760. Inv. No. Ker 4028

78 Giovanni da Bologna. Born 1529 in Douai, died in Florence 1608. *Allegory of Architecture.* Bronze, hollow casting, reddish-brown lacquer, yellowish-brown natural patina. Height 34.5 cm. Florence, about 1570 to 1580. Inv. No. 57/54

79 Bustelli. *Bust of Count Sigmund von Haimhausen.* Porcelain, partly painted and gilded. Height 45 cm. Nymphenburg, about 1761. Inv. No. Ker 4369

80 Ignaz Günther. Born 1725 in Altmannstein (Upper Palatinate), died in Munich 1775. *House Madonna.* In oak, uncoated. Height 75 cm. About 1761/62. Formerly on Günther's dwelling-house in Munich. Inv. No. 53/2

81 Cosmas Damian Asam. Born 1686 in Benediktbeuern, died in Weltenburg monastery 1739. *Self-portrait.* Oil on canvas. Height 91 cm., width 71 cm. About 1720. Inv. No. R 7498

82 Giuseppe Sammartino. *Domestic Nativity Crib.* Terracotta, painted. Height of figures 73 cm. Naples, about 1790. Presented 1892 as part of a collection belonging to the Councillor of Commerce Max Schmederer, Munich. Inv. No. Krippe 48

COLLECTIONS OF CLASSICAL ART
AND GLYPTOTHEK

The reopening of its two houses on the Königsplatz will bring together the Munich collections of Greek and Roman antiquities. The venerable edifice of the Glyptothek will once again house the collection of sculptures, when the reconstruction of its interior is completed. The building opposite, on the south side of the square, which was erected between 1838 and 1848 by G. F. Ziebland on the commission of Ludwig I to house the "Exhibition of Arts and Industry" and which finally became the New State Gallery, has, from the autumn of 1966, taken up its new rôle of housing the Collections of Classical Art. Under this name, formerly the "Museum of Minor Works of Classical Art", there will be combined in an appropriate setting the famous collection of Greek vases, the collections of Greek and Roman terracottas and bronzes, and the collection of gold and glass.

More than any other of the Munich collections the Glyptothek and the Classical Collections owe their world-wide fame to the taste of their founder and patron, the Crown Prince, later King Ludwig I of Bavaria.

Influenced by the general neo-classic ideals of his time, it was his first journey to Italy in the winter of 1804/05 which, in his own words, opened the eyes of this eighteen-year-old youth to classical art. In the course of this journey he decided to assemble, at his own expense, a collection of original Greek and Roman works of art. During his stay in Rome he negotiated the first purchases and then charged his agents in Rome to continue the work. The acquisitions of important items from the possessions of Roman and Veronese nobility were negotiated by J. G. Dillis between 1809 and 1811.

It contributed greatly to the success of his plans when in 1810 the Crown Prince entrusted the purchase of classical works of art to the Würzburg sculptor Johann Martin Wagner, a discriminating connoisseur and an able negotiator. Wagner had considerable means at his disposal, and on the breaking up of collections within the houses of Roman nobility, he had the opportunity to select those items of the finest quality which best contributed to make a well-balanced collection. The Crown Prince followed the success of his project in a lively exchange of letters. In the years between 1810 and 1814 Wagner, with the help of his friends, the sculptors Canova and Thorvaldsen, succeeded in amassing an impressive number of classical sculptures. The first shipment of fifty chests left for Munich in September 1814, to be followed in 1819 by the *Barberini Faun* which had been acquired with the utmost difficulty in 1813.

Meanwhile Crown Prince Ludwig had himself made further purchases. Through his participation in the Congress of Vienna he acquired in 1814 from a private owner in Vienna the Greek torso known as *Ilioneus*. Other important acquisitions followed during his stay in Paris in 1815. On the occasion of the break up of the Napoleonic collections Dillis and Leo von Klenze took over about forty valuable works of classical art from collections which had once belonged to Cardinal Fesch and to Prince Albani in Rome as well as to the Palazzo Bevilacqua in Verona.

While the classical sculptures from the Italian collections were, with certain outstanding exceptions, mainly copies of classical works done in the Imperial Age, the first original works of art from Greece were obtained for Ludwig by the Nuremberg architect Haller von Hallerstein, whom he had commissioned in 1811 to make purchases and to carry out excavations. It was also Hallerstein whose work in Greece eventually brought the pediment figures from the Temple of Aegina to Munich. In May 1811, together with the English architect Cockerell, he was engaged in architectonic investigations and excavations around the ruined temple on the island. During the course of these they unexpectedly came upon the comparatively well preserved sculptures from both pediments of the temple. The torsos and fragments of the *Aeginetans* were recovered and brought by way of Athens to the island of Zakynthos, and thence on to Malta. Wagner, who had been sent out by Crown Prince Ludwig, only saw casts of the sculptures in Athens, but in 1813 he was able to procure the *Aeginetans* for the prince. In 1815 he had them removed from Malta via Naples to Rome. There, in the studio of the Danish sculptor Thorvaldsen, they were restored in marble under Wagner's supervision. For this purpose models made by Thorvaldsen were used. The restored *Aeginetans* finally reached Munich in 1828.

After 1814, by which time the collection of sculptures had grown to a considerable size, Crown Prince Ludwig initiated the building of a separate museum. Between 1816 and 1830 a noble, generously appointed building was erected on the newly laid out Königsplatz, to plans of his master-builder Leo von Klenze. While the building was being constructed, acquisitions were in effect limited to the filling of the spaces shown to be free in the plans of the architect. The building and the arrangement of the collection, which taken together, form an artistic achievement which at that time ranked as unique, were completed and opened in 1830 under the name of the "Glyptothek".

The art treasures within the Glyptothek were further increased in the course of time, by Ludwig himself through his purchase in 1853 of the *Youth of Tenea*, and by acquisitions made by the Bavarian State since the beginning of the twentieth century, including the purchase in 1910 of the second great archaic *Figure of a Youth* and a number of outstanding Greek burial monuments. The Glyptothek is indebted to the Bavarian Society of Friends of Art and to a number of private donors for a series of other masterpieces which it owns today.

Greek vases had been well-known since the beginning of the eighteenth century. They came principally from excavations in Sicily and Lower Italy and soon were included in all the collections of classical art. In learned treatises and books with full plates they were valued as evidence regarding the life and beliefs of the Greeks, but also as examples of Greek painting.

But it was a personal achievement far beyond this when Ludwig decided to place at the front of the gallery of paintings in the Pinakothek he had planned, a representative collection of Greek vases as an introduction to European painting. It was certainly with this in mind that he had acquired in 1824 the first Greek vases from the Panettieri collection in Agrigento, including the famous Sappho vase. New possibilities presented themselves when, after the discovery of the Etruscan necropoli in 1828, the landowners of the district around Vulci took to excavation with great zeal. In 1831 Wagner managed to acquire for the king the extensive collection of vases owned by the Candelori brothers. 51 choice vases including the Execias bowl and the Andocides amphora which had been the property of Lucien Bonaparte (Principe Canino), as well as his valuable collection of Etruscan gold jewellery, were bought at auction after his death by Professor Thiersch in Frankfurt in 1841. To these was added a collection of vases from Lower Italy, gold jewellery and silverware from the estate of Caroline Murat, the former Queen of Naples, and later "Countess Lipona". The inclusion of the collection of the English traveller and painter Dodwell who lived in Rome, added, apart from some archaic vases found in Greece, a valuable find of Etruscan bronzes from Perugia, Greek figures in clay and Roman goblets. The collection of the Norwegian sculptor Fogelberg provided clay figures from Lower Italy and Roman lamps. In the summer of 1841 King Ludwig summoned Wagner to Munich from Rome to direct the arrangement of the collection of vases on the ground floor of the Pinakothek which had been opened in 1836.

The remaining classical art treasures (bronzes, terracottas, goblets, gold jewellery) formed part of the "Combined Collections" within the old art gallery building in the Court garden from 1844 to 1869.

There existed in Munich a further collection of antiquities which dated back to a venerable past: the "Antiquarium" which Duke Albrecht V had founded in the Residence. It comprised a great number of portrait busts, mostly Roman, some of them originals and some copies. They were arranged in a sumptuous, barrel-vaulted chamber, built in 1563 in the Renaissance style. It had been strongly influenced by Italian models, though it already bore a marked personal stamp. In addition, the prince, with the help of the 37

Fugger family from Augsburg, had brought together a fine collection of smaller classical treasures, particularly bronze statuettes and tools, which were housed together with all kinds of curiosities in the ducal *Kunstkammer*, which later became the Mint. The first considerable additions to the Antiquarium did not come until 1803 when the cabinet of antiquities belonging to the Elector Karl Theodor was brought from Mannheim to Munich. In 1808 the bronzes which until then had been kept in the *Kunstkammer*, were transferred to the Antiquarium. Following the secularisation, the collection of Steiglehner, the last Prince-Abbot of St. Emmeram in Regensburg, fell to the Bavarian State in 1813, and in 1817 that of Count Thun, the Bishop of Passau, was also incorporated in the Antiquarium. In 1826 the collection was further enriched by the addition of the Greek vases from the estate of King Maximilian I Joseph, and in 1839 by Greek terracottas from the collection of the architect Gärtner. From time to time archaeological discoveries of the Roman period in Bavaria were also included.

After the death of King Ludwig I the movable items from the Antiquarium, together with antiquities from the Combined Collections, were put on exhibition in 1869, under the title of the "Royal Antiqua-rium" in the gallery on the Königsplatz, but in 1872 they had to be moved again to the ground floor of the New Pinakothek. Finally after the First World War, the Antiquarium and the collection of vases were combined to form the "Museum of Minor Works of Classical Art" on the ground floor of the Old Pinakothek. The collections from the private estate of King Ludwig formed the basis and main substance of this museum. Its possessions were increased by various gifts, particularly from the Museum Society, by the large collection of the archaeologist Paul Arndt in 1908, and in 1929 thanks to the Lutz bequest. Since 1890 varied and regular acquisitions financed by the Bavarian State have supplemented and strengthened the collection. The most valuable additions were in 1934 and 1957, when the collections of antiquities belonging to James Loeb and Baron Hans von Schoen were transferred to the museum as gifts. At the express wish of the donors, each is exhibited as a separate collection.

The items from the Glyptothek Collection and the Collections of Classical Art, as far as they had been owned by the king, became in 1918 the property of the Wittelsbach settlement trust (*Wittelsbacher Ausgleichsfonds*). In this way they were preserved for public exhibition.

DESCRIPTION OF ILLUSTRATIONS

85 *Marble Statue of a Youth.* Found at Tenea near Corinth. About 550 B.C. Height 153 cm. The statue was discovered above the burial place of a man, whose name was certainly inscribed on the plinth which is lost. Acquired 1853. Glypt. No. 168

86 *Warrior from the East Pediment of the Temple of Aphaia at Aegina.* About 490 B.C. Height of detail 34 cm. The helmeted, bearded head belongs to the figure of a warrior who, shot by an arrow, has fallen to the ground in his death struggle. The figure is among the best preserved figures of warriors from both pediments. It belongs to the left corner of the east section of the temple pediment. Next to this figure and to the right, towards the centre of the gable, there followed in turn a kneeling bowman, then an unarmed man coming to the help of a falling warrior, and finally the latter's opponent, a warrior standing upright. A similar group of five warriors on the other side of the centre, on the right half of the pediment, mirrors this arrangement. The position in the centre of the pediment is taken by the figure of Athene. Considerable amounts of nine out of the total of eleven pediment figures are preserved. The decorative figures from the west pediment are in a much better state of preservation. Now housed in the Glyptothek, there are ten almost complete torsos out of thirteen, five of which still have the heads. Both groups represent Aeginetan heroes in combat at the conquest of Troy. Athene, and in the east pediment Heracles as an archer, assist the Greeks. It is possible to infer from stylistic variations that the group on the east pediment was not added until about 490 B.C. to that of the west pediment which dates from 510 B.C.

87 a) *Head of Homer.* Marble reproduction made in the Imperial Age, copied from a bronze statue of the poet of about 450 B.C. Height 36 cm. The original head must have been a famous work of an unknown master, since several copies have survived. There is no record of his name. The closed eyes and mouth slightly open as if about to speak were, in the style of that time, the typical indications of blindness. Its interpretation as a portrait of the old and according to the legend blind Homer is beyond doubt. Presented to the Glyptothek 1892. Glypt. No. 273

87 b) *Head of the Medusa.* Marble copy from the Imperial Age of an original of the 5th century B.C. Height 38 cm.

38

The head which Goethe admired when it was still in the Palazzo Rondanini at Rome is worked in high relief, and certainly belongs within a larger context. It can reasonably be assumed that the original work adorned the centre of the shield, approximately 4 m. high, on the immense gold and ivory statue of the Athene in the Parthenon at Athens by the sculptor Phidias. Acquired from the estate of Rondanini 1810. Glypt. No. 252

88 *Tomb Relief of Mnesarete*. Found in Attica. About 380 B.C. Pentelic marble, height 163 cm. The inscription carved on the ornamentation above the relief informs us that this is the tomb of a young woman, Mnesarete, who on her death left behind her mother, husband, brothers and a child of tender age. Following the classical rule, the dead woman is represented together with her maid, and, as mistress of the house, is seated. Presented to the Glyptothek 1910. Glypt. No. 491

89 a) *Head of Aphrodite*. Outstanding copy of a head from an original marble statue of the early 3rd century B.C. (called the Capitoline Venus) which is now lost. Height 39 cm. The statue of this youthful goddess must have resembled the famous Cnidian statue of Aphrodite stepping from the bath, by Praxiteles. Acquired 1816. Glypt. No. 479

89 b) *Sleeping Satyr* (called the Barberini Faun). About 220 B.C. Height of detail 43 cm. The end of the nose and the elbows have been repaired in modern times. Leaves and fruit of the vine-garland in the hair have been damaged. This sculpture of the sleeping satyr, leaning against a rock with one arm curved above his head, was found between 1624 and 1641 as a torso, but with an almost undamaged head near the Castle of S. Angelo in Rome. Soon after it was skilfully restored and provided with a new plinth by Bernini. As a classical work of art the satyr was greatly admired in the Palazzo Barberini where it stood until 1799. Acquired from the Barberini estate 1813. Glypt. No. 218

90 a) *Bronze Statuette of Poseidon*. Late 2nd century B.C. Height 30.5 cm. In a commanding attitude, holding the trident, Poseidon is represented as ruler of the elements. The right lower leg and foot, and left foot are recent. Reed garlands in the hair damaged; the original trident is lost. Inv. Slg. Loeb 15

90 b) *Golden Diadem*. Consisting of a central section in the form of a knot, and curved side sections inlaid with garnets and with pendants set with stones. Found in a grave in Southern Russia as burial jewellery. Macedonian-Greek filigree work of the 4th/3rd centuries B.C. Length 44 cm. Above the central section a winged goddess worked in gold foil, flanked by sea-horses. Inv. Slg. Loeb 589

91 *Marble Bust of Augustus* wearing the civic crown. From the second quarter of the 1st century. Height 54 cm. The civic crown, made of leaves and fruit of the oak – from that time on the prerogative of Roman Emperors – was conferred by the Senate in the year 27 B.C. upon the young Octavian, victor and conqueror in the civil wars, who thereafter was called "Augustus". He is represented as he was then at 36 years of age. But the style of the work suggests that it was carried out some decades after the death of the Emperor. Acquired 1815 from Verona. Glypt. No. 317

92 a) *Attic Amphora*. From Attica. Early 8th century B.C. Height 51 cm. Outstanding work of the mature period of geometric vase painting. The whole vessel is covered with a richly developed succession of ornaments. Here we see the first stages in the depiction of living beings (geese, bucks resting, grazing deer), from which was to develop the wealth of pictorial illustrations on Greek pottery. Acquired 1907. Inv. No. 6080

92 b) *Jug from Rhodes with Animal Friezes*. About 630 B.C. Height 32.5 cm. In early Greek times individual styles were developed not only in Athens but also in Corinth, Rhodes and other islands of the Aegean Sea. This jug from Rhodes has on a light ground a pattern of buds and blossoms rising from the base, and above this two broad pictorial friezes: on the middle section grazing roebucks, on the shoulder geese, roebucks and a pair of mythical griffons. Acquired 1911. Inv. No. 6212

93 a) *Attic Mixing Vessel with Bung-hole*. Found in Sicily. 480–470 B.C. Height 52.5 cm. The unbroken state in which the vessel has been preserved is unique. The elongated figures of the principal illustration are designated by inscription as Alcaeus and Sappho. Acquired 1824. Inv. No. 2416

93 b) *Attic Amphora by the Andocides Painter*. From Vulci. About 520 B.C. Height 54 cm. The new "red-figure" style of painting was developed by the Andocides painter (named after the potter Andocides), a pupil of Execias, about 530 B.C. On the back of this vessel a picture by the hand of another painter in a traditional "black-figure" technique is placed as if in deliberate contrast to the picture by the master illustrated here. The theme of the two paintings is the same with only slight variations, namely that of Hercules enthroned on Olympus in the company of Athene. Acquired 1841. Inv. No. 2301

94 *Attic Drinking Bowl by Execias*. From Vulci. About 530 B.C. Diameter 30 cm., height 13 cm. The bowl is the work of the potter and vessel painter Execias, who was working in Athens between 550 and 525 B.C.: on the edge of the base of the bowl is painted "Execias made it". Within the hollow of the bowl there is a "black-figure" painting, for once as an exception on a background coloured coral red. It illustrates Dionysus crossing the sea. The poetic composition of the picture combines the appearance of the god among the Greeks with the legend in which the god, having fallen unrecognised into the hands of pirates, causes a vine to spring from the mast of the boat and transforms the mariners into dolphins. The bowl has been restored from fragments; the white of the sails has partly flaked off, and the profile of Dionysus has partly been lost by splintering. Acquired 1841. Inv. No. 8729

EGYPTIAN COLLECTION

The Egyptian Collection of the Bavarian State had its first beginnings in the Antiquarium of Duke Albrecht (1550 to 1579). While he was still Crown Prince, King Ludwig I (1825 to 1848) began to prepare the ground for a representative collection of Egyptian art in Munich by making purchases in Rome from amongst the art treasures which Napoleon I had previously carried off from Rome to Paris, and later by acquisitions from the collections of Sieber, Michel, Dodwell, Drovetti and Ferlini. These Egyptian works of art were divided between three Munich collections: statues and reliefs were placed in the "Egyptian Hall" of the Glyptothek as an introduction to the Greek and Roman marbles; the minor works of Egyptian art, mainly items made of metal or glass, were placed in the Museum of Minor Works of Classical Art, while items bearing inscriptions such as stelae and papyri, as well as sarcophagi, mummies and burial furniture, made up a separate Egyptian section within the "Combined Collections" under the care of the Bavarian Academy of Science. In 1935 the Egyptian Collection was separated from the Combined Collections and, with the addition of several items lent by the Glyptothek, was exhibited in the Residence as the State Collection of Egyptian Art. Its exhibition rooms were destroyed during the war. In recent times all the Egyptian items in the possession of the Bavarian State were brought together in the Egyptian Collection. The work of conserving the pieces, which suffered as a result of being in storage during the war, has not yet been completed. Because of the lack of space it will be possible to show in the immediate future only a selection from the large stock of items.

Up to the most recent times additions have been made to the Egyptian Collection, particularly through the gifts of Professor Friedrich Wilhelm Freiherr von Bissing, made between 1906 and 1914, through the presentation of archaeological finds by the German Oriental Society, the Administration of Egyptian Antiquities and other archaeologists, through bequests such as the collection of Senator Doctor honoris causa Wilhelm Esch, 1961, and by purchases, amongst others of the collection of Professor Mirko G. Roš in 1963.

It is the intention of the Egyptian Collection through original works of art to present a clear picture of the ancient culture of the Nile from its beginnings and throughout the 3,000 years of its development as an example of an ancient culture and art within its own historical framework. The decisive step which this people took into the self-created order of their historical existence was based upon their faith in a divine scheme of the universe. The guarantor of this scheme was the divine king of the Two Lands, Upper and Lower Egypt, and the most perfect expression of this order was reached on more than one occasion, namely in the great epoch of the Old Kingdom (2660 to 2160 B.C.), in that of the Middle Kingdom (2040 to 1785 B.C.), in the New Empire (1550 to 1085 B.C.) and finally in the Late Period (1st millennium B.C.). Since the first foundation of the Kingdom (about 3000 B.C.) the visual arts had been almost exclusively at the service of this religious order whose requirements they formulated and immortalised in temples, palaces and funeral buildings, in statues, murals, inscriptions and implements, for the life in this world and in that to come. Each Egyptian work of art bears as an expression of this order its own truth within itself; its construction is ordained according to set proportions, and during the three thousand years of Pharaonic art these remained almost unchanged. Within the limits set to the technique of representation in sculpture, relief, painting and script, the matter depicted varied according to the historical changes of the period.

The temporary housing of the Egyptian Collection on the ground floor of the house at No. 10 Meiserstrasse, will combine within the rooms available the statues and reliefs, shown as far as possible in historical sequence; the painted sarcophagi, the figures from tombs, the burial furniture of various periods, jewellery, scarabaei and amulets, bronze figures, glass and faience ware, papyri and writing materials will on the other hand be grouped according to subject.

Flint implements from the early and middle Stone Age, found in the further reaches of the Nile valley and in the western oases, mark the path taken by the prehistoric nomads from the steppes, later the deserts, to the well-watered valley of the Nile. With the settling of the tribes in the Nile valley towards the end of the late Stone Age (5th/4th millennium B.C.) the first works of art of ceramic and other materials were made. All the principal types of late prehistoric culture are represented in the Munich collection: the red-polished vessels with a black rim or with painting in white, the round pots with representations of ships on a light ground, stone palettes in various forms used for grinding down eye cosmetic, neck ornaments, figurines of deities and decorative hair-combs made of bone. Round vessels and shallow dishes in hard coloured stone provide links with the art of the period of the unification of the Kingdoms, the beginning of Egyptian history (about 3000 B.C.).

The sudden stimulus given to the arts at the time of the first Egyptian kings known to history is illustrated in the animal figures with a greenish glaze, in figure carvings in ivory, and in the statuette of a woman in limestone; the discovery of the hieroglyphic script and the art of relief are exemplified by a tombstone from Abydos and by the limestone tablet with the representation of a woman seated at a dining table, which came from the district of Memphis.

The first main flowering of Egyptian art in the Old Kingdom can be studied in statues and numerous reliefs from royal and private burial places and from a shrine of the Sun-god. A family group, the statue of a court flautist and the figure of a servant kneading dough, illustrate the character of Egyptian burial sculpture in its "unilinear", well-proportioned construction. The head of a life-size statue of the Sun-god in human shape, wearing the head cloth of a king with the disc of the sun, made of brown quartzite, is unique evidence of sun worship in the 5th dynasty (about 2400 B.C.). The development of relief carving in the residence at Memphis can be followed in early examples found in the tomb of Achtihotep and in samples of the technique of painted plaster from the tomb of Prince Neferma'at as well as in reliefs from tombs dating towards the end of the Old Kingdom.

Of the art of the Middle Kingdom, the time of the second peak of artistic achievement, the Munich collection owns specimens of reliefs from the funeral temple in Thebes of King Mentuhotep, the founder of the new epoch. Statues mostly small in size, made of stone or copper, represent courtiers and members of the middle classes of the 12th and 13th dynasties. A head of Sesostris III in light brown quartzite is representative of a group of statues of kings of the late 12th dynasty, where the expression seems to be marked with an awareness of the heavy responsibilities of kingship.

The Munich collection is particularly rich in memorial stones to the dead bearing representations in relief and inscriptions; from the time of the Middle Kingdom they were set up in the Holy Domain of Osiris, the god of death, at Abydos.

Treasures of the New Empire, in which the Pharaonic Empire reached the summit of its power, are represented by the monumental Lion's Head from the Delta area which was acquired in 1964. It comes from a sculpture of the lion god who, with commanding and ferocious gaze, guarded the open north east boundary of Egypt. The small idealised image of King Amenhotep II (1437 to 1410 B.C.) is an example of the mature art of the 18th dynasty.

The torso of a man, part of a family group in black granite speckled in white, is a masterpiece which shows the extreme refinement and intensity of which Egyptian art concerned with the sun worship of King Amenhotep IV (Ikhnaton) was capable. A head, larger than life-size, and a torso of King Ramses II, the statue of the falcon-headed god Horus, the lion-headed goddess Sekhmet and the huge head of the god Ptah of Memphis all belong to the 19th dynasty. There are two family groups of the same period, the smaller still showing the original paint. The most important exhibit in the Munich collection, however, is the great block figure of the high priest of Amun and director of the entire work of building the 41

Amun temple at Karnak, Bekenchons. The biographical inscriptions on the front, the base and the back pillar of this statue are historically very important. The head of the statue follows the ideal form of the time of Amenhotep III.

The expressive art of the religious reformer Amenhotep IV (Ikhnaton) can be seen in numerous fragments from his Shrine to the Sun at Karnak and from his residence at Amarna. The wall from the tomb of Amenmône, chief of the craftsmen and the goldsmiths, is well worthy of comparison with the torso of a man mentioned above as a masterpiece of the later 18th dynasty. A relief representation of Ramses II making sacrifice, from a pillar in quartzite, and a door lintel with representations of King Osorkon before several gods, are examples of the official art of the time.

The Munich collection illustrates clearly the refinements which came about in the life of the New Empire in the artistically fashioned instruments for the toilet, in painted earthenware wine pitchers, in jewellery and in ornaments made of semi-precious stones, of glass and faience.

The art of coloured enamelling and glazing which flourished from the early 18th dynasty, around 1500 B.C., is particularly well represented by the famous goblet made of opaque glass bearing in enamel the name of Thutmose III, and by other glass vessels as well as the important collection of glazed tiles with inscriptions on the borders or representational scenes from the palace of Ramses II near Quantîr in the Eastern Delta (bequest of Senator Doctor h.c. Wilhelm Esch). Mention must also be made of the curved sword decorated with gold inlay from the collection of weapons, which was amongst archaeological discoveries at Sichem in Palestine.

An important representation of an old man in brown quartzite belongs to the late Egyptian era (1st millennium B.C.), as well as a series of idealised representations which illustrate the development of portraiture from the 7th century to about 300 B.C. Noteworthy among the portraits of the kings is a plaster head of unusually individual character, probably representing Nectanebos I who belonged to the last native (the 30th) dynasty. Later heads of kings show how the traditional Egyptian forms gradually degenerated under the Ptolemies and up to the time of Roman rule.

The old Egyptian forms, the survival of which was being endangered by the infiltration of Hellenistic art forms into the Nile valley, were preserved in "instructional" sculptures of the early 3rd century B.C., on which the lines of the proportions were marked out. These "sculptor's models" and some unfinished statuettes in the Munich collection illustrate the working methods of the Egyptian sculptors.

Occasionally the extraneous Hellenistic art forms combined with the Egyptian; an outstanding product of this "hybrid art" is represented by the priest's head with two flower buds in the hair, executed probably in Alexandria in the 1st century B.C. by an Egyptian sculptor. Part of the back pillar which remains behind the head shows that this portrait head, purely Hellenistic in form, belonged to a statue which was wholly Egyptian in conception.

The acceptance by the Greek and Roman colonists of the Egyptian mummification and burial customs led to the production of plaster masks and mummy portraits in tempera or encaustic painting, which are well represented in the Munich collection. The Hellenistic-Egyptian cults which spread from Alexandria throughout the whole ancient world, produced the head of the god Serapis and the small, expressive stone figure of the mother goddess Isis, with the Horus child on her lap.

The Emperor Hadrian's enthusiasm for Egypt gave rise to the copy of the Egyptian "Kanopos" erected at his villa in Tivoli near Rome; from its ornamentation, the collection possesses a series of statues which were worked in Italy in imitation of the Egyptian style. The obelisk in granite, bearing a hieroglyphic inscription, which had been set up by a Roman official, also came to the Munich collection from Rome.

The valuable gold jewellery of a queen of Meroë comes from early Roman times, and the finger rings and bracelets show, even as late as this, the continuing influence of inherited Egyptian forms.

In Roman times classical forms displaced more and more the native Egyptian ones and provided the basis for the Christian art of the Nile valley. The coloured tombstone of a devotee of Isis, and an approximately contemporary one of a youth with a cross, illustrate the closeness of heathendom and Christianity at that time.

DESCRIPTION OF ILLUSTRATIONS

97 *Lion's Head*. From El-Dab'a in the East Delta. New Empire, 18th dynasty, about 1450 B.C. Limestone with traces of former painting. Height 68 cm. Fragment of sculpture, above life-size, of a lion-god who holds off the enemies of Egypt on the north east border of the country. The commanding power of the Egyptian lion is expressed in the "wild look" of the eyes and the majestic modelling of the closed jaw. Acquired 1964. Inv. ÄS 5348

98 a) *Fragment of a Relief* from the cult chamber of Achtihotep. From Memphis (Saqqara Cemetery). Early Old Kingdom, end of 3rd dynasty, about 2600 B.C. Limestone, originally painted. Height 61 cm., width 71 cm. Priests of the dead supply the ritual gifts of water and sacrifices to the statues of their dead master on the right and left, now largely broken off. Acquired 1959. Inv. ÄS 4854

98 b) *Wall Fragment with Coloured Paste Inlays* from the cult chamber of Prince Neferma'at. From the burial place at Medûm. Old Kingdom, beginning of 4th dynasty, about 2550 B.C. Limestone with inlays. Height 45 cm., width 50 cm. One ox is grazing on reeds, another is guided by a herdsman. The figures are sunk into the surface of the stone and filled out with coloured pastes (the pastes in this fragment have for the most part been renewed). Presented by Freiherr von Bissing. Inv. Glypt. 103

99 *Figure of a Servant kneading Dough*. From the excavations of the burial place near the pyramids of Gizeh. Late Old Kingdom, 6th dynasty, about 2300 B.C. Limestone, originally painted. Height 26 cm. Grave furniture for the care of the dead man in the next life. Acquired 1960. Inv. ÄS 4862

100 *Part of a Wall*. From Memphis (Cemetery at Saqqara). New Empire, end of 18th dynasty, about 1340 B.C. Limestone, originally painted. Two details of relief illustrations from the tomb of the chief of the craftsmen and goldsmiths, Amen-mône:

a) Amen-mône and his wife (kneeling) are served with food and cool water by the tree goddess (not preserved) from her abode in the palm and sycamore trees, and having taken on the form of two spirit-birds, drink from the pond in the shade of the two trees. Height of detail 32 cm., width 51 cm.

b) The couple in the rich, fashionable dress of the New Empire, are seated at the dining table. Height of detail 51 cm., width 28 cm. Presented by Freiherr von Bissing. Inv. Glypt. 298

101 *The Block Figure of Prince Bekenchons*, high priest of Amun and director of the entire work of building the Amun temple. Probably from the temple district of Karnak (Thebes). New Empire, 19th dynasty, about 1230 B.C. Hard limestone. Height 138 cm. The figure (the *Würfelhocker*) with drawn-up knees, crouching on the ground and completely swathed except for the head and hands in a smooth garment, carries inscriptions of great historical interest. In the sacrificial formula on the front is the prayer of Bekenchons, that his name may be immortal in Thebes. In the plinth inscription Bekenchons hopes to be fortunate enough to live for 110 years. In the inscription on the back pillar he enumerates the stages in his career in office, from his childhood in the reign of Sethos I (1302-1290 B.C.) up to and during the reign of Ramses II (1290-1224 B.C.), covering a total of 75 years. Furthermore he estimates the exact number of years until his promotion to the next position. He speaks with pride of having built the turret portals of a temple and obelisks in granite, as well as having made high flag poles and having built the barque of the gods Amun, Mut and Chons. Acquired by King Ludwig I 1823. Inv. Glypt. (*Wittelsbacher Ausgleichsfonds*) 38

102 *Statue of the God Horus*. Found in the 17th century during the erection of the monastery Alla Minerva in Rome on the site of the Shrine of Isis. New Empire, 19th dynasty. Black syenite. Height of detail 47 cm., over-all height 163 cm. The transition from falcon head to human body is discreetly concealed under the long hair of the god. Originally erected in a temple of Ramses II in central Egypt, brought to Rome in Roman Imperial times. Acquired by King Ludwig I 1815. Inv. Glypt. (*Wittelsbacher Ausgleichsfonds*) 22

103 *Head of a Priest*. From Dime, Faijûm. Black syenite. Height 34 cm. This significant head in black Egyptian hard stone was broken from a statue, above life-size, of purely Egyptian composition with a back pillar. The head in Greek-Hellenistic style, with beard and hair arrangement belonging to the same style, and two flower buds in the hair as mark of priesthood, is the work of an Egyptian sculptor. Inv. Glypt. 30

104 *Burial Stone of a Devotee of Isis*. From the Greek town of Antinoë in central Egypt. 4th century A.D. Limestone, bearing the original paint. Height 42 cm. The boy, within a niche, is squatting on a cushion, and the attitude as well as the addition of the bunch of grapes and the small dog indicate that he is a worshipper of the goddess Isis. Acquired 1960. Inv. ÄS 4860

RESIDENCE MUSEUM AND TREASURY

Over the centuries the former seat of the Bavarian dukes, electors and kings developed from a late medieval moated castle to an almost bewildering complex of buildings spread round six large courtyards. In the extent of its growth and the varied nature of the individual buildings, the Residence in its final form resembles the community of a small city. The princely patronage of art which, stretching out far beyond the boundaries of the small country, was able to combine autochthonal continuity with all that was new in foreign cultures, found its earliest expression in the humanistic world of Duke Albrecht V. The Antiquarium was built in 1570, to plans drawn up by Jacopo Strada, as a worthy setting for a collection of classical sculptures; the oldest section of the present buildings is therefore one of the earliest museum buildings north of the Alps. Since that time every ruler made additions to the Residence and alterations to what had been handed down. Already in 1644 it was said to be "more an Imperial than a Ducal palace". It was rarely that the museum form of exhibition was chosen for movable works of art. Only special collections were brought together in small apartments. Otherwise the individual works of art made their appearance as integrating components of a total decorative scheme, giving expression to and providing a foil for the elevated style of court life. For this reason, as both a building of architectural interest and a museum, the Residence can claim a special place among the public collections of art in Munich.

It was only in 1920, two years after the end of the monarchy, that this first and most important hoard of Wittelsbach works of art was made accessible to the public. Although the princes of the nineteenth century waived their right to many works of art, for the benefit of newly established museums and galleries, the Residence Museum was nevertheless the most comprehensive museum of the art of interior decoration in existence. The irreplaceable buildings with their original examples of late Renaissance, Rococo and Neo-classic architecture were badly affected during the Second World War. However, the movable exhibits and the rich possessions of paintings, sculptures, tapestries, pieces of furniture, porcelain and works of goldsmith's art escaped any drastic losses. Reconstruction is not yet complete. But the building has been so far restored as to recreate the distinguished appearance of its original form. Apart from the task of preserving those parts of the building that remained intact, the first intention is to re-establish the incomparable harmony which existed between the rooms and the works of art they contained. Only in this way will it be possible for the particular magic of the many and varied objects of art to be seen once again to their best advantage. Here we can indicate its abundant riches only in a few examples. They will have to stand as representatives of the originality and value of whole spheres of art.

Amongst the paintings there are allegorical representations from the early Baroque period, views of towns and landscapes, as well as portraits of princes of the eighteenth century, minutely painted battle scenes from the Napoleonic Wars, portraits in *Biedermeier* style, and grandiose Italian landscapes. A charming addition to these paintings by artists such as Sandrart, Vivien, Desmarées, Belotto, Hess and Stieler is a wide selection of miniatures by German and Netherlandish masters of the sixteenth to eighteenth centuries, including delightful works of Paul Brill, Hans Bol, Johann König, Matthias Kager, Joseph Werner and Maximilian de Geer.

In the sphere of sculpture the collection of marble busts acquired by Duke Albrecht has been already 44 mentioned in connection with the Antiquarium. It includes excellent works from the time of the Roman Emperors and the Italian Renaissance. The late Renaissance is represented by the impressive bronze sculptures of Hubert Gerhard and Hans Krumper. In addition there are carved figures by Johann B. Straub from the time of Bavarian Rococo, and Classicism is represented by the marble statue of a *Venus italica* by Antonio Canova.

The collection of tapestries in the Munich Residence is among the largest in the world. The *St. Paul Cycle* worked in gold and silver thread, which came from a Brussels factory, goes back to Pieter Cocke van Aelst. From the early seventeenth century there are the *Artemisia Tapestries* made in the First Paris Factory under Frans van den Planken from sketches by Henri Lerambert, and the cycles worked in gold thread of *The Months*, *The Grotesques* and *The Deeds of the Count Palatinate Otto von Wittelsbach* designed by Peter Candid and made in the First Munich Factory under Hans van der Biest, who also produced the *Series of Heroes*, made in Enghien. The eleven Persian tapestries called the *Polish Tapestries* after the Polish princess Anna Maria Constanze belong to a slightly later period. The hangings worked from cartoons of Lambert de Hondt representing a series of scenes from military campaigns are from the Brussels factory of Hieronymus Le Clerk and Jaspers van der Borght and are dated 1696. The most valuable textile products of the eighteenth century are the *Great Mogul Cycle* of tapestries and the *Hunting Cycle* designed by Jean B. Oudry from the Beauvais factory. Finally there are the delicately coloured *Rinaldo and Armida Cycle* of tapestries designed by Charles Coypel and made in 1762 at the Paris factory of Jacques Neilson, as well as a series illustrating the *History of the Dukes of Bavaria* from the Second Munich Factory, and the knotted tapestries made in 1765 and 1775 in the Mannheim and Heidelberg Savonnerie factory.

The high artistic quality of the furnishing contributes equally to the appearance of the rooms. There are state tables of the early seventeenth century with outstanding panels of intarsia work in precious stones which probably came from Augsburg or Munich. Skilfully made boulle cabinets and tables with engraved inlays of brass, silver and mother-of-pearl in tortoise-shell date back to about 1680 to 1700. The elegantly carved and gilded console tables and sets of chairs from the Munich workshops in the style of Joseph Effner and François de Cuvilliés the Elder, are in complete harmony with the panelling of the same period in the "Ancestral Gallery" and the *Reiche Zimmer*. The finest achievements in the European art of ebony work in the eighteenth century are represented by outstanding works by Charles Cressent, François Oeben and David Roentgen. The splendid writing tables, secretaires, chests of drawers, corner cupboards and French clocks decorated with marquetry and lacquer panels are mostly ornamented with French bronze metal work. The particular splendour of these rooms is enhanced by porcelain vases, chandeliers and wall-lights in silver, gilded bronze and crystal.

The ceramic works mainly belong to special collections. The majolica pieces acquired by Albrecht V include works from the Faenza and Urbino factories (with paintings by Leonardo di Ascanio Bettisi). Within the Collection of East Asiatic Porcelain there are Chinese works of the late Ming and Chien lung dynasties and Japanese Arita and Kakiemon ware. The Porcelain Chambers contain porcelain figures and sets of table-ware which were made in Europe during the eighteenth century. Amongst the white and decorated porcelain from factories such as Meissen, Frankenthal, Nymphenburg and Sèvres, there are enchanting works by Johann Jakob Kändler, Johann Wilhelm Lanz and Franz Anton Bustelli.

The table-plate used at the courts of the princes is kept in the Silver Chambers. Since the older exhibits were lost in the War of the Spanish Succession, this particularly extensive collection comprises mainly work of the eighteenth and early nineteenth centuries from Munich, Augsburg, Strassburg and Paris.

In addition to this silver there are two collections from the sphere of sacred art. In the *Paramentenkammern* we find some particularly notable robes and antipendia of the seventeenth and eighteenth centuries from amongst the rich possessions of the former court chapels, including work in damask and silk brocade and embroidery in gold thread, plain embroidery and appliqué work. In contrast to these exhibits which were first put on view in 1958, the Chamber of Reliquaries contains an old collection of religious relics which originally belonged to the *Reiche Kapelle*. The richness of the settings worked in gold of the late Renaissance and of the eighteenth century

45

was a measure of the great esteem in which these relics were held.

The importance even of these sacred exhibits is surpassed by the world-renowned Treasury, newly housed in ten rooms on the ground floor of the Königsbau. Far beyond its material value, this venerable collection of precious possessions handed down through generations of princely households, represents the jewel of the rich collections of art in the Munich Residence.

Duke Albrecht V founded this entailed estate four hundred years ago. During the following centuries the princes' zeal for collecting brought a great variety of additions, and it was further enlarged after 1777, on the union of the Bavarian and Palatine lines of the Wittelsbachs, by the addition of the Palatine treasure and after 1803 by works from the secularised cathedral and monastery foundations. It includes insignia of sovereignty and religious works ranging from early to late medieval times, devotional objects and precious table-ware from the Renaissance, including an outstanding collection of rock-crystal by Milanese masters, sets of toilet articles and luncheon sets, personal jewellery and badges of orders of the Baroque and Empire periods, the crown jewels of the Bavarian kings and exotic works from the sixteenth to eighteenth centuries. In its richly varied examples of the art of the goldsmith and the carver of gems through a millennium of western civilisation the treasure of the House of Wittelsbach – like the Residence as a whole – represents an incomparable monument to princely patronage.

DESCRIPTION OF ILLUSTRATIONS

107 Hubert Gerhard. Born about 1550 in Hertogenbosch in the Netherlands, died in Munich 1620. *Allegory of "Bavaria"*. Cast in bronze. Height 231 cm. Munich, about 1590. Originally a garden sculpture (on a fountain), 1615 to 1943 as decorative figure on the cupola of the temple in the Munich Court garden.

108 a) *Tapestry "Stag Hunt"*. Design by Jean B. Oudry. Wool. Height 357 cm., width 500 cm. About 1727. From a hunting cycle from the Beauvais factory (under Noël Antoine Le Mérou). Inv. No. W 108

108 b) *Tapestry "Rinaldo's Farewell"*. Design by Charles Coypel. Wool. Height 155 cm., width 355 cm. 1762. From a "Rinaldo and Armida" series from the First Parisian Gobelin Factory (under Jacques Neilson). Inv. No.W 4110

109 *Tapestry "Reception of a Greek Embassy"*. Design by Peter Candid. Wool with gold thread. Height 407 cm., width 645 cm. About 1610. From a series "The Deeds of the Count Palatine Otto von Wittelsbach" from the First Munich Gobelin Factory (under Hans van der Biest). Inv. No. W 2

110 François Oeben. Born about 1715 in Germany, died in Paris 1763. *Secretaire*. Inlay work in coloured woods; gilded bronze fittings. Height 148 cm., width 105 cm., depth 40 cm. Paris, about 1760. Inv. No. M 436

111 George Desmarées. Born 1697 in Österby (Sweden), died in Munich 1776. *Portrait of Elector Max III Joseph of Bavaria with his Commissary Count Seeau*. Oil on canvas. Height 192 cm., width 149 cm. Signed and dated 1755 at lower right. Inv. No. G 955

112 a) *Silver Tureen*. Strassburg inspector's mark 1725 to 1730, master's mark Johann Ludwig Imlin the Younger. Height 21 cm., width 19 cm. Inv. No. Sik 6418

112 b) *Portable Wine Casket of Silver*. Paris inspector's mark 1712/13, master's mark Claude Ballin the Younger. Height 33.5 cm., width 38 cm. Inv. No. Sik 2525

113 *"Fo-Dog"*. Chinese porcelain (émail sur biscuit with turquoise- and aubergine-coloured glazing) of the K'ang Hsi dynasty; gilded bronze mounting. Height 49 cm. About 1715. Inv. No. PVb 781

114 a) *Pendant* (with half-length figure of Cleopatra). Gold, gold enamel and precious stones. Height 8.7 cm., width 6.9 cm. German, about 1590, with Upper Italian gem-carving, about 1550. Inv. No. Sch 642

114 b) *Portrait Medallion* (probably Duke Philipp the Good of Burgundy). Gold, gold enamel, chalcedony. Diameter 9 cm. Burgundian, about 1440. Inv. No. Sch 19

114 c) *Eagle Cameo*. The oval onyx plate is set into the lid of a golden box from Germany (probably Vienna) of about 1720. Length of the box 9 cm., width 7 cm., height 2 cm. Gem-carving from the Hohenstaufen period, about 1230. Inv. No. Sch 11

114 d) *Double Eagle*. Gold, gold enamel, diamonds, rubies, pearls. Height 15.6 cm., width 11 cm. Viennese or Italian, about 1550. Inv. No. Sch 49

115 a) *Crown of Empress Kunigunde*. Gold, gold filigree, precious stones, molten glass, pearls. Height 5 cm., diameter 19 cm. Lorraine, about 1010. In 1803 the crown of Emperor Heinrich II's wife came from Bamberg to Munich. Inv. No. Sch 10

115 b) *Crown of an English Queen*. Gold, gold enamel, sapphires, rubies, emeralds and pearls. Height 17 cm., diameter 18 cm. Probably from Prague, about 1370. Probably Princess Anne of Bohemia, wife of Richard II of England, brought this crown from Prague to England. The crown is known to have been in the possession of the King of England in 1399. Inv. No. Sch 16

116 *Statuette of the Knight St. George*. Gold, gold enamel, gilded silver, diamonds, rubies, emeralds and pearls. Head, neck, legs and tail of the horse are carved in agate. Height 50 cm., width 34.2 cm., depth 19,8 cm. Figure probably from Munich, about 1590; base of gilded silver by Stephan Noetzer, after 1622. Inv. No. Sch 58

117 *French Clock*. Case with tortoise-shell veneer and gilded bronze fitting by Charles Cressent or his circle; works by Etienne Leroy. Height 23.2 cm. Paris, about 1740. Presented by King Louis XV of France to Elector Karl Albert of Bavaria. Inv. No. M 163

118 a) Franz Anton Bustelli. Born 1723 in Locarno, died in Munich 1763. *Porcelain Figure "The Cheese-seller"*. Height 16.8 cm. From the Nymphenburg factory, about 1755. Inv. No. P I 234

118 b) *Quatrefoil Porcelain Dish*. Length 32 cm., width 25.5 cm. Part of the "Birds" service from the Frankenthal factory, 1771. Inv. No. P 1857

119 *Lidded Bowl*. Rock-crystal, gold, gold enamel, precious stones, pearls. Height 16 cm., diameter 19 cm. Vessel of the early 14th century; decoration of gold (after a sketch by Hans Holbein the Younger) of about 1540. Known to have been in Westminster Palace and the Upper Jewel Hall in the Tower of London from the middle of the 16th century to 1649, since 1711 in the treasure of the Elector of the Palatinate in Düsseldorf. Inv. No. Sch 40

120 *Miniature Ciborium of King Arnulf of Carinthia*. Gold, precious stones, oak. Height 59 cm., width 31 cm., depth 24 cm. Probably Reims, after 893. This late Carolingian ciborium of a portable altar was a gift to the St. Emmeram monastery in Regensburg from Arnulf of Carinthia before he was crowned German Emperor in 896. Came to the Reiche Kapelle in Munich 1811. Inv. No. Sch 5

121 *Reliquary Monstrance* (detail). Silver cast, gold enamel, precious stones, pearls. Total height 115 cm., total width 37.5 cm. Probably Augsburg, 1592 (probably by Matthäus Wallbaum or Heinrich Winterstein). Known to have been on the high altar of the Reiche Kapelle since 1611. Inv. No. R K 32

122 *Cope from the Polling Robes of Office* (detail). Gold and silk embroidery. Total height 145 cm., total width 455 cm. Southern Germany (probably Munich), about 1725. From the former Augustinian monastery at Polling (Upper Bavaria). Since 1814 in the Residence. Inv. No. 4

123 Joseph Stieler. Born 1781 in Mainz, died in Munich 1858. *Four Portraits from the Gallery of Beauties of King Ludwig I*. Oil on canvas. Height 71 cm., width 59 cm.
a) Catharina Botzaris (1841), married Prince Georg Karadjas 1845. Inv. No. G 396
b) Auguste Strobl (1827), married Anton Hilber 1831. Inv. No. G 372
c) Helene Sedlmayer (1831), married valet Miller 1832. Inv. No. G 384
d) Amalie von Schintling (1831). Inv. No. G 383

124 Annibale Fontana. Born about 1540, died 1587 in Milan. *Amphora* (so-called Jason vase). Rock-crystal, gold mounting, rubies. The figure on the lid (Neptune) in gold cast. Total height 41.5 cm., width 31.5 cm., depth 17.5 cm. Milan, about 1570. The figure frieze shows scenes from the myth of Jason. Inv. No. Sch 322

125 Hans Reimer. Born in Schwerin, died in 1604. *Ceremonial Goblet* (detail). Gold, gold enamel, sapphires. Total height 48.6 cm., diameter (base) 12.7 cm. Munich, 1563. Perhaps made after sketches by Hans Muelich (1516–1573). Inv. No. Sch 562

126 *Ivory Chest*. Ivory, gold mounting with rubies and sapphires. Height 18 cm., width 30 cm., depth 16 cm. Ceylon, middle of the 16th century. The ivory reliefs show scenes from the time of the Great King Bhuvaneka Bahu (1521–1551). Inv. No. Sch 1247

MUSEUM OF ETHNOLOGY

The State Museum of Ethnology which originated in a collection of curiosities owned by the Wittelsbachs, and into which, in the course of time, the most varied collections have been incorporated, celebrated its centenary in 1968.

Particularly noteworthy, amongst those sections which later developed into the most important features of the museum, is the Brazilian collection of the two scientists Spix and Martius, the former a zoologist and the latter a botanist, who as members of the Bavarian Academy of Science, on the instigation of King Max Joseph, in 1819 and 1820 made a journey up the Amazon and established an ethnographical collection. The store of the items from South America was later increased by the collection of Princess Therese of Bavaria, and by the Peruvian items added by Professor Ubbelohde-Doering (director of the museum from 1936 to 1957). He also acquired the Aztec sculpture in wood illustrated here and the cloak from Peru. And so both the advanced civilisations of South America as well as the primitive cultures of the Amazon basin are exemplified in the museum.

The exhibits from Africa and the Pacific are of a high quality but are rather few in number. Those which are connected with the Cameroons and New Guinea are for the most part the gifts of former German colonial officials, and the rest of them are some of the acquisitions made by Professor Max Buchner, director of the museum from 1887 to 1907.

Noteworthy is a small collection of Benin bronzes, including the panther shown in the illustration (plate 137) which Ubbelohde-Doering acquired in 1952.

Buchner also enriched the Asiatic section of the museum by the purchases which he was able to make on the occasion of a journey round the world in the years 1889 and 1890 particularly in Japan and Indonesia.

Numerous Asiatic objects in the museum date back to the Ingolstadt Jesuit Father Ferdinand Orban (1652–1732) who worked in China. His collection contains small art objects of that time. It was housed at first in the University of Erlangen and only later brought to Munich. The basis of the section of Indian art comes from the collection of the French traveller Lamare Picquot, who visited West Africa, the Cape of Good Hope and particularly India. This collection was acquired by King Ludwig in 1841. In 1865 part of the Japanese collection of Philipp Franz von Siebold (1796–1866), a doctor and naturalist from Würzburg who between 1823 and 1830 worked in Japan, was also bought by Ludwig. Finally the Asiatic section of the museum was increased by the collection of Schlagintweit and de Grez and supplemented by the acquisitions from Indo-China, which Professor Lucian Scherman (director of the museum from 1907 to 1936) made on a journey to Asia in 1910/11, and by the purchase of a part of the Thailand collection of Karl Döhring, an engineer who worked in Thailand from 1906 to 1911. The latter collection contains lacquered work, paintings and wood-carvings from Thailand, while Scherman collected principally carvings in wood and woven fabrics from Burma. The textiles of the Indo-Chinese advanced cultures and of the more primitive tribes are abundantly represented in his collection. It was also Scherman who bought the Somaskanda group, a bronze sculpture from India.

In 1957 Professor Preetorius transferred to the Bavarian State his East Asian collection which consisted mainly of Chinese and Japanese graphic art and painting. The collection was exhibited for the first time in its entirety in the museum in 1958 under

48

the title *The Art of the East – the Preetorius Collection*. It has its own very special place amongst the items of the State Museum of Ethnology.

For a long time now the stress in this museum has been more on "art" than on "ethnography"; but that does not mean that ethnography has been in any way neglected. Ludwig Bachhofer who was in charge of the Asiatic collections of the museum from 1922 to 1935, held the same view as Scherman, the director at that time, that "the art of non-European peoples could not be separated from their ethnography, because only through familiarity with the general cultural conditions and limitations of these peoples, could be found the true measure of their artistic achievements". Today the rich collections as well as pictorial archives provide the ethnographical background to the works of art on exhibition. While forty years ago, the collections of Scherman and Ubbelohde-Doering had tended to give the museum largely the character of a museum of art, the acquisition of the Preetorius collection clearly stamped it as a museum of the art of non-European peoples and cultures; and this really means all the non-European cultures, for the State Museum of Ethnology in Munich exhibits both the art of the highly developed civilisations such as that of India, China, Japan and Peru, and the art of the so-called primitive societies, such as that of Africa, Australia or South America.

It had been usual in art exhibitions to consider only the so-called higher cultures and to leave aside or to give scant attention to the so-called primitive cultures as being inferior achievements less worthy of consideration. This has changed only in most recent times with the recognition that the artistic achievements of the primitive peoples can very well stand comparison with those of the more advanced civilisations, and indeed often surpass them. The misunderstanding of unfamiliar and in particular of primitive cultures comes to no small extent from the attempt to understand those cultures too exclusively through their techniques and the tools with which they worked, without at the same time gaining understanding of them through their artistic works and indeed looking upon these as the more important.

The advanced civilisations such as those of China, India or America express themselves almost exclusively through their grandiose works of art. Primitive civilisations appear in a false, even wretched light if they are merely represented by the tools they employed and not by the art which they produced.

This brings us to one of the aims of a modern ethnological museum which is to correct the ideas held in Europe and elsewhere about the intellectual world of the so-called primitives and to provide an adequate picture of the cultural development of early man.

Our understanding of the development is insufficient. In a curious way the lines of artistic development do not seem to run parallel to those of general cultural "progress". They coincide at various points in history only to separate again later. Certainly an exhibition of Australian art illustrates a high artistic level amongst men whose material culture is of the utmost poverty. In spite of all the intensive European study of non-European civilisations there still exists on this very point a widely held misconception: the underestimation of the primitives. It is the task of the museums of ethnology to correct this misconception. There is no means more suited to illustrate the greatness and importance of primitive cultures than the representation of their art.

The State Museum of Ethnology has since the end of the war sought to do justice to this task in a series of special exhibitions in which the most diverse cultures in the world were presented. Catalogues were published for each of these exhibitions, often richly illustrated. In this book are shown some of the finest exhibits from amongst the extensive possessions of the museum, most of which were amassed during the travels of individual scholars, from the late eighteenth century up to the present day, and which today afford us a survey over the entire range of non-European cultures and their art.

DESCRIPTION OF ILLUSTRATIONS

129 *Winter Landscape*. China. Li Shih-hsing, dated T'ai-ting ping yin (1326). Indian ink on silk. Size 135 × 53 cm. According to Ludwig Bachhofer the signature is a later addition and the picture can be assumed to be one of the rare works from the 11th century. Preetorius collection.

130 *The God Shiva*. Bronze sculpture from Southern India. About 1050–1100. Height 50 cm. The god is seated upon a rectangular base. He wears a high crown (jatâ-mukuta), his belt is decorated at the front with a lion's mask (kîrti-mukha). His lower right hand makes the gesture

denoting fearlessness (abhaya-mudrâ), the lower left hand holds an unidentifiable, button-shaped object. The upper left hand carries a small antelope, the emblem from the upper right hand, an axe, is missing. Mus. No. Kr 62, Slg. Scherman

131 *Detail from an Indian Folding Altar*. Orissa. About 1800. Painted wood. Height 49 cm., width 34 cm. Above, Krishna in the chariot of Nanda; Yasodâ leading Krishna away, and Krishna sucking at the breast of the demoness Pûtanâ. In the central section, on the outside to the left and right is Krishna overcoming the wrestler Cânûra, and subduing the elephant of King Kansâ, in the centre Krishna slaying the demon Bakâsura in the shape of a crane. In the lower section, Krishna breaking the butter pot of Yasodâ, and Krishna with a snake standing before the bed of a woman. Mus. No. 57–14–1

132 *Detail of a Wooden Sculpture*, of a so-called roof ornament, from the island of New Caledonia. 19th century. Total height 222 cm., detail 63 cm. Deeply worked anthropomorphic carving, painted red, still made with stone tools. Mus. No. 10468

133 *Head of a Demon*. Persian work. 19th century. Iron. Total height 34 cm. The surface of the iron head has been covered all over with gold and silver – mostly surface damaskeening; plants, animals and illustrative scenes, damaskeening partly lost; one ear missing. Mus. No. 13–81–3

134 *Detail of a Cloak in Tapestry Technique*. Nazca valleys, South Peru, coastal Tiahuanaco civilisation. About 700–900. Height 103 cm. The abstract motif is the so-called "tiger's eye motif": puma or jaguar heads with large, black and white eyes, with the mark of a falling tear; teeth represented by two canine teeth near the tear track and the nose, which is simplified to a rectangle, alternate with graduated or winged volutes in each of which the tiger's eye motif is suggested twice. Mus. No. X 448

135 *Detail of Carving* on an oar blade from New Zealand. 18th century. Total length 174 cm., length of detail 25 cm. The highly abstract figure represents a mythological monster. Mus. No. 34–38–1

136 *Human Head in Wood*. One end of a tongue instrument (Aztec: teponaztli). Place of origin unknown, upland valley of Mexico, Aztec. 14th century. Blackened wood. Height 18 cm. The eyes are inlaid with pieces of shell. Mus. No. 51–20–1

137 *Figure of a Panther*. Benin, Nigeria. 16th century. Bronze. Height 43 cm., length 16 cm. Mus. No. 52–7–1

138 *Wooden Sculpture from the Baluba Tribe*. Congo, Africa. 19th century. Height 37 cm. The woman represented, seated, with a vessel, is a so-called Kabila figure, a motif today not accurately definable, which was very widespread in the eastern Congo. Mus. No. 13–57–147

139 *Seated Athlete*. Sculpture from Guatemala. 15th century. Blackish-grey clay. Height 28.5 cm. Exact place of origin unknown, probably Quiché district. Mus. No. 12–70–8

140 *Shark*. Costa Rica, Quepo and Koto civilisation. 14th century. Gold. Weight 175 g., size 12.5 cm. The tail raised high, fins lightly notched; solid, the belly-side hollowed out. Mus. No. 14–43–1

When on 15th March 1963 the rooms of the State Coin Collection within the venerable Munich Residence were opened to the public, it marked a unique addition to the Munich museums of art. The doors were opened on an almost four-hundred-year-old Bavarian collection of coins, medals, plaques, gems and cameos. It comprised a unique store of riches in glyptics and the art of die-sinking, from classical times up to the present day, as well as a great number of portrait medals from all the European countries, including some of the best works of the Renaissance and Baroque. Gold and silver, as well as bronze and lead in fine castings with a splendid patina, offered a picture of the greatest richness, for which the simple exhibition furnishings and the lacquered show cases, which had previously been used as coin cabinets, provided a fitting frame.

The history of the collection dates back to the sixteenth century. Although there was no official foundation charter, it is to Duke Albrecht the Magnanimous (1550 to 1579), the first great princely collector in Bavaria who founded the *Kunstkammer* and the Court library, that we are indebted for the foundation of the coin collection. He was a man with great interest in art and history, who took up the collection of classical coins about 1560 and subsequently bought two large private collections. Along with the famous library of Johann Jakob Fugger he purchased also his coin collection, and acquired the collection of the Bishop of Augsburg, Johann Egolf von Knöringen, from the University of Ingolstadt, to which it had shortly before been presented. In building up his collection he was supported by men of wide classical scholarship, such as the much-travelled Dutch engraver Hubert Goltzius and the widely cultured Jacopo Strada, both distinguished artists who had written numerous works on classical numismatics. There was also the Dutch physician Samuel Quichelberg, the author of the oldest work on the methodology of museums and collections of rarities, and the first director of the *Kunstkammer* and the coin collection. Later Albrecht also acquired the collection of the Salzburg prebendary Johann Fickler.

The numismatic collection appears to have continued without any further important additions by purchases, until the reign of the Elector Maximilian III Joseph. But it would be right to assume that from the time of Maximilian I to that of Karl Albert a considerable extension of the collection took place, on the one hand through the addition of the many sets of their own Bavarian coins and medals, and on the other through the lively exchange of these with the coins of other European princely houses.

Up to this time the growing princely coin collection, as the private treasure of the Electoral house, was no more than a part of the princely image. But with the establishment of the Bavarian Academy of Science in 1759 it took on more the aspect of an academic foundation. Maximilian III Joseph made the collection into a public institution of the State, associated with the Academy, by removing it from the private ownership of the princes; there consequently followed the task of "bringing the coin and medal collection into better order and arranging it in a truly systematic way". At the same time the growth of the collection gained new impetus. Considerable additions were made on the accession of the Elector Karl Theodor, who brought his valuable Palatine collection from Mannheim to Munich. The gem collection in particular was increased by the collection of the Abbot Coelestin Steiglehner of St. Emmeram in Regensburg, and in 1815 the unique collection of Salzburg coins and medals from the Abbey of

St. Peter in Salzburg was bought. After 1803 the secularisation of the Bavarian monasteries brought considerable additions.

Ludwig I particularly encouraged the growth of the classical section of the coin collection. While he was Crown Prince, he took a passionate interest in Greek numismatics, and on his travels in Italy he was intent on increasing the contents of the coin cabinet. In particular the purchase of four great collections of Greek and Roman coins raised the cabinet to the level of international importance; these were the Cousinéry, Astuto, Longo and Avellino collections. Other important acquisitions were those of the two Bavarica collections of the Maltese Chancellor Friedrich Woschitka and of the Landshut numismatist J. P. Beierlein.

Later in the nineteenth and in the twentieth centuries the section containing German and Italian medals of the Renaissance was successfully extended, as well as the coins of the German Middle Ages and modern art medals principally of the Munich school. In recent times it has been possible to bring the Oriental section to a high standard by the purchase of a complete collection and by systematic consolidation, while the acquisition of the glyptic collection of the Munich archaeologist Paul Arndt gave international importance to the collection of engraved gems.

When the coin collection was moved in 1960 to the Residence, it was returning to its former home, from which it had been moved for a short time in 1782 to a building in the Schwabinger Gasse, today the Theatinerstrasse, which then housed the Academy and Court library. After its rehousing in the Residence, the collection was moved to the building of the old Jesuit College which was then the Academy of Science, where it stayed until the destruction of the building in the Second World War in 1944. After the war it was temporarily housed until 1960 in the so-called Gallery Buildings on the Arcisstrasse, later the Meiserstrasse.

DESCRIPTION OF ILLUSTRATIONS

Classical Coins and Engraved Gems

143 1. Athens, Attica. *Tetradrachma*, about 510 B.C.
Obv.: head of Athena wearing helmet, from the right.
Rev.: owl to the right in quadratum incusum, in the left upper corner of which is an olive branch.
Legend: A Θ E
Weight: 17.23 g. silver

2. Syracuse, Sicily. *Tetradrachma*, about 410 B.C.
Obv.: head of the fountain nymph Arethusa surrounded by four sporting dolphins, almost frontal, on the hair-band the die-sinker's signature KIMΩN
Legend: ΑΡΕΘΟΣΑ above the beaded circlet
Rev.: quadriga in front of an overturned winning-post to the left, above it, Nike with wreath, below, an ear of corn.
Legend: ΣΥΡΑΚΟΣΙΩΝ
Weight: 17.18 g. silver

3. *Scarabaeus*, late 6th century B.C.
Young helmet-smith sitting at his work. Rock-crystal

4. *Cask-shaped Gem*, 5th century B.C.
Heron, standing to the right. Agate

144 1. Miletus, Ionia. *Stater*, about 600 B.C.
Obv.: bull and lion, back to back.
Rev.: three quadrata incusa.
Weight: 13.96 g. electron

2. Ephesus, Ionia. *Stater*, 6th century B.C.
Obv.: cow, suckling calf, to the right.
Rev.: quadratum incusum.
Weight: 13.95 g. electron

3. Acragas, Sicily. *Decadrachma*, about 410 B.C.
Obv.: quadriga to the left, above it an eagle.
Legend: ΑΚΡΑΓΑΣ
Rev.: two eagles gorging a hare lying on rocks, to the left; in the field on the right, a cicada.
Weight: 43.21 g. silver

4. Septimius Severus, Emperor 193–211 A.D. *Aureus*, Rome, 202 A.D.
Obv.: bust of Septimius Severus, wearing armour, crowned with laurel wreath, from the right, within beaded circlet.
Legend: SEVER P AVG PM TRP X COS III
Rev.: Julia Domna, wife of the Emperor, between the sons Caracalla with laurel wreath (left) and Geta (right), beaded circlet.
Legend: FELICITAS SAECVLI
Weight: 7.02 g. gold

5. Constantine I, Emperor 306–337 A.D. *Medal*, Ticinum (Pavia), about 315 A.D.
Obv.: armoured bust of the Emperor with helmet (with monogram of the Greek name of Christ), shield and lance, holding saddled horse with right hand, almost frontal, beaded circlet.
Legend: IMP CONSTANTINVS PF AVG
Rev.: the Emperor, crowned by Victoria, addresses soldiers from a platform.
Legend: SALVS REI PVBLICAE
Weight: 6.40 g. silver

6. Achaios, viceroy in Asia Minor 220–213 B.C. *Stater*, Sardis.

Obv.: draped bust of the king wearing diadem from the right, within beaded circlet.
Weight: 8.50 g. gold

7. Hadrian, Emperor 117–138 A.D. *Sestertius*, Rome, 125–128 A.D.
Obv.: head of Hadrian with wreath of corn and small drapery, to the right, within beaded circlet.
Legend: HADRIANVS AVGVSTVS
Rev.: Artemis with bow and arrow, standing, to the right, beaded circlet.
Legend: COS III S-C
Weight: 26.10 g. brass

8. India, the Sultan of Malwa, Mahmud III. 1435–1469. *Presentation Coin* of 5 tankas from the year A. H. 868 (= 1463/64 A.D.)
Weight: 55.38 g. gold

European Coins of 9th–16th Centuries

145 1. Emperor Ludwig the Pious, 814–840. *Gold Solidus* without date of minting, place of mint unknown.
Obv.: head of Emperor from the right, wearing laurel wreath.
Rev.: cross within wreath of leaves.
Weight: 4.38 g. gold

2. Germany, King Philipp, 1198–1208 or Otto IV, 1198–1215. *One-sided Silver Pfennig*, about 1210, minted in Augsburg or Donauwörth. Facing bust of the sovereign with crown, sceptre and orb. Illustration in size of the original.
Weight: 0.69 g. silver

3. Falkenstein in the Harz, Count Burkhard II, 1142–1174. *One-sided Silver Pfennig*, about 1170–1180, coined in the Ermsleben mint.
Standing falcon, from the right, surrounded by several-towered buildings. Illustration in size of the original.
Weight: 0.66 g. silver

4. Bavaria, Duke Albrecht V, 1550–1579. *Ducat* without date stamp, minted in Munich.
Obv.: bust of the Duke, from the left, with covered head.
Rev.: Bavarian coat of arms.
Weight: 7.1 g. gold

5. Imperial city of Augsburg. *Quadruple Taler* of 1625.
Obv.: view of town, above it two angels with coat of arms of town, the cedar-nut.
Rev.: one-headed Imperial eagle with crown, sceptre, sword and orb.
Weight: 116.42 g. silver

6. Archbishopric of Salzburg, Archbishop Wolfgang Theoderich von Raitenau-Langenstein, 1587–1612. *Medal* with value of 6 talers (six-edged clip), minted in 1593 in Salzburg on the occasion of the return of the Salzburg troops from the Turkish campaign.
Obv.: St. Rudbert and coat of arms.
Rev.: tower threatened by hail, storm and waves.
Weight: 172.45 g. silver, gilded

7. Aragon, King Ferdinand II the Catholic, 1479–1516. *Ten-ducat piece*, without date stamp, minted in Saragossa.
Obv.: bust of king, crowned, from the left.
Rev.: Coat of arms of Aragon.
Weight: 35.04 g. gold

8. Dauphiny, France, King François I, 1515–1547. *Quadruple Teston*, minted in 1537 in Romans.
Obv.: bust of king, crowned, from the left.
Rev.: coat of arms of Dauphiny, France.
Weight: 38.36 g. silver

9. Duchy of Milan, Emperor Karl V (Duke of Milan 1535–1556). *Ducatone*, without date of minting.
Obv.: bust of Emperor.
Rev.: St. Augustine kneeling before St. Ambrose.
Weight: 33.73 g. silver

146 1. Germany, King Philipp, 1198–1208 or Otto IV, 1198–1218. *One-sided Silver Pfennig*, about 1210, minted in Augsburg or Donauwörth. Facing bust of the sovereign with crown, sceptre and orb. Illustration three times enlarged (see pl. 145, 2).
Weight: 0.69 g. silver

2. Falkenstein in the Harz, Count Burkhard II, 1142–1174. *One-sided Silver Pfennig*, about 1170–1180, coined in the Ermsleben mint.
Standing falcon from the right, surrounded by several-towered buildings. Illustration three times enlarged (see pl. 145, 3).
Weight: 0.66 g. silver

3. *Cameo* with figure of sovereign enthroned between two angels. Italy, 13th century.
41 × 51 mm. (without mounting), three-layered sardonyx.

European Medals

146 4. *Gilded Bronze Medal* in the honour of Anne of Brittany, wife of Charles VIII of France, and the Dauphin Charles-Orland. Presentation medal of the city of Vienne, 1494. By an unknown artist.
Diameter: 76 mm.

147 1. *Model for a Medal*. No legend; portrait of a stout man; on evidence of another medal he is to be identified as Count Christoph von Nellenburg und Thengen. About 1535. Made by the medallist Friedrich Hagenauer, born in Strassburg, active mainly in Augsburg and on the Lower Rhine.
Diameter: 91 mm., maple wood

2. *Model for a Medal* with portrait of a Nuremberg patrician, Hieronymus Holzschuher. Dated 1529. By the Nuremberg medallist Matthes Gebel.
Diameter: 42 mm., Solnhofen stone

3. *Model for a Medal* with portrait of 28-year-old Peter Resch, probably member of an Ulm family. Dated 1530. By Christoph Weiditz, medallist and goldsmith, active mainly in Augsburg; accompanied Karl V to Spain and Italy.
Diameter: 57 mm., box-wood

4. *Golden Jewel* in enamelled setting worked in gold with portrait of Elector Maximilian I of Bavaria; coat of arms on reverse, not illustrated. Made in 1623/24. Work of a Munich die-sinker, probably Paul Zeggin.
41 × 51 mm. without setting

5. *Bronze Medal* with portrait of Count Palatine Georg von Speier. Dated 1520. On reverse, figure of Spes, with hands raised in prayer. By the Augsburg medallist and carver Hans Schwarz who was active in South Germany, France, Poland and Denmark.
Diameter: 68 mm.

6. *Bronze Medal* with opposed portraits of Duke Wilhelm V of Bavaria and his consort Renate. Dated 1585. By Hubert Gerhard or one of his close associates of the Munich school. The text of 13 lines on the reverse not illustrated, refers to the laying of the foundation-stone of the Munich Jesuit Church of St. Michael.
Diameter: 79 mm.

148 1. *Lead Medal* with portrait of the Prince-Abbot of Kempten, Albert von Hoheneck, 1584–1587, with coat of arms on reverse. By Valentin Maler, medallist, wax-modeller and goldsmith in Nuremberg.
Diameter: 61 mm.

2. *Bronze Medal* with portrait of Domenico Malatesta Novello, Lord of Cesena; on the reverse, the figure of a young knight, dismounted from his horse, kneeling embracing a crucifix. Made about 1445 by Antonio Pisano, known as Pisanello, the creator of the Italian Renaissance medal.
Diameter: 86 mm.

3. *Silver Medal* with portrait of Mary Tudor, daughter of Henry VIII of England and wife of Philip II of Spain; on the reverse, a female allegorical figure bearing palm and olive branches and a torch. Struck in 1555. By the Milan sculptor, medallist and gem-carver Jacopo da Trezzo, who also worked in the Netherlands and Spain.
Diameter: 66 mm.

The Munich City Museum was founded in 1874 by the Municipal Council, and opened in 1888 in what had been the arsenal, musketry store and granary of the city. This first museum building dates back to the early sixteenth century. Very close by lived the sculptor Ignaz Günther and the painter Carl Spitzweg.

Between 1926 and 1928 and 1930 and 1931, when Dr. Eberhard Hanfstaengl and Konrad Schiessl were the directors, reconstruction and new building was carried out, but in 1944 the museum was badly damaged by bombs. Fortunately the contents had been removed to safety, and were not badly damaged. In 1954 part of the museum was opened again. Since 1960 large extensions built in the area between Oberanger-, Rosental-, and Nieserstrasse have created a modern museum building which will subsequently be completed by further additions.

Within the new and the old buildings are housed the City Museum together with its related collections, the Photographic and Film Museum, the Puppet Theatre Collection, the Collection of Musical Instruments and the German Brewery Museum.

One of the tasks of the City Museum is to preserve, evaluate and exhibit material that illustrates the civic and social history of Munich. The scope of the collections includes every aspect of the life of the town, house and home, national costume and fashion, trades and handicrafts, customs, religious life and festivals. The collection of graphic art which illustrates the topography and civic history of Munich contains today some 150,000 pictures, and includes the Maillinger, Zettler, Rehlen, Schwanthaler and Proebst collections. There are also paintings and posters, some 10,000 portraits and 15,000 coins and medals; in addition there are archives of photographs, transparencies and newspaper cuttings, and a technical library.

The museum illustrates the history of Munich in a series of sections which fit together chronologically like the cubes of a mosaic to form the total picture of the growth and development of the town. Immediately beside the entrance there is the Primitive History Section. It has been developed in cooperation with the State Prehistoric Collection which has lent many of the exhibits. These range from the neolithic age to the immigration of the Bajuvari and through a wealth of illustrations give us an insight into the people and their way of life in past ages. The Sandtner town model from the year 1572 shows a picture true to the smallest detail of the lay-out of the streets and the arrangement of the houses in medieval and post-medieval Munich. The model (a copy double the size of the original in the Bavarian National Museum) which has a diameter of four metres, is so arranged that the spectator has a bird's eye view of the town. Views and models of the old town fortifications complete the representation. From here the visitor moves to the admirable spaciousness of the former Armoury (*Zeughalle*). It is the finest late Gothic hall in the city and has remained unchanged for more than four hundred years. The famous *Maruska Dancers* (morris dancers) by Erasmus Grasser, dating from the year 1480, are presented here in such a way that for the first time the full measure of their beauty is evident. Exhibits illustrating personal and community life establish links between the various periods. The exhibition called *Munich Plans and Builds* organised and kept up to date by the Press and Information Office, forms a bridge to the present time and affords a glimpse of the future. This exhibition gives information by means of models, plans and enlarged photographs, regarding current objectives in town planning, traffic problems and private and public building. In connection with the exhibition, lectures and discussions are held on these present-day problems.

The section *Domestic Life in Munich from 1700 to 1900* is of particular interest. In its suite of 25 rooms fitted out to illustrate the social history of the times, it recreates the pattern of life in old Munich. This section is to be extended considerably to include examples of interiors from the art nouveau period down to the present day. Other exhibitions are being prepared dealing with *The Three Generation House* and *The World of Toys* with a play section. A collection of Turkish textiles and embroideries presented by Melek Lampé has provided the starting point for a future section of folk art.

In addition to presenting the permanent sections which recreate the picture of the town and the life of its citizens, the City Museum has other functions. Frequently special exhibitions are mounted to maintain a sense of vitality in the museum. In constantly changing arrangements the old is related to the new. To make this possible the museum has in part turned away from the usual static methods to a dynamic principle which continually draws new visitors to a rapid succession of exhibitions on the most varied cultural themes. In addition to themes concerned expressly with Munich, the range of subjects is deliberately broadened to cover a very wide field.

With the completion of the already existing and the newly planned buildings (along the Jakobsplatz and the Sebastiansplatz) it will be possible to coordinate more closely the work of the separate sections and of the related institutes within the museum area, and to make the Munich City Museum into a centre of education and exciting discovery.

DESCRIPTION OF ILLUSTRATIONS

151 *Eagle from the Chain* of the former Company of the Munich Crossbow and Musketry Marksmen. Silver. Height 12 cm., width 9 cm. Second half of 15th century. It is the oldest of the insignia that have been fastened to the chain by the Bavarian dukes to mark memorable occasions. Inv. No. VIII 1/3

152 Abraham Zeggin. Son of a Munich goldsmith, and accepted into guild in 1586, died 1617. *Skull of the Blessed Nantwein Mounted as a Chalice.* Silver, gilded. Height 19 cm., width 13 cm. 1609. Munich inspector's mark. The feast day of the Blessed Nantwein (Nantwin) is celebrated on 7th August. He was a pilgrim of unknown origin, and according to tradition, he died at the stake in 1286 near Wolfratshausen, Isar valley, after false accusations. On the site of his martyrdom, called St. Nantwein, a church was built in 1290 and became a place of pilgrimage. Wine was offered to the pilgrims from the mounted skull. Inv. No. 36/2049

153 a) Erasmus Grasser. Born 1450 in Schmidmühlen (Upper Palatinate), died in Munich about 1518. *Munich City-arms.* Limewood, coating renewed. Height 43 cm., width 36 cm. Recorded 1477. This carving is one of the earliest authenticated works by Grasser, made in 1477 for the banqueting hall of the Old Munich Town Hall.

153 b) Domenico Quaglio. Born 1786 or 1787 in Munich, died in Hohenschwangau 1837. *View of the Old Munich Town Hall* with the Talburgtor tower. Oil on canvas. Height 70 cm., width 90 cm. About 1825. Inv. No. 30/1679

154 Grasser. *Maruska Dancer* (morris dancer). Limewood, worked in the round, coating renewed. Height 75 cm. Revorded 1480. One of a series of 16 dancers, made by Grasser in 1480 for the banqueting hall of the Old Town Hall. Ten figures have survived and are exhibited today in the Munich City Museum. Inv. No. 50/488

155 Franz Anton Bustelli. Born 1723 in Locarno, died in Munich 1763. *Saint John from a Crucifixion Group.* Porcelain, glazed white. Height 48 cm. Recorded 1756. The master's mark, missing on the other known models of St. John, suggest that the St. John figure in the Munich City Museum is the first execution of the model, made in 1756. Inv. No. E 1206

156 a) Hermann Obrist. Born 1863 in Kilchberg near Zurich, died in Munich 1927. *Large Wall-hanging* "Wild cyclamen" (called "Lash" by Fuchs: "Pan" 1896). Silk embroidery – satin stitch on woollen material. Height 119.5 cm., width 183.5 cm. 1895. Inv. No. 49/63

156 b) Gertraud von Schnellenbühel. Born 1878 in Jena, living in Weimar. *Table Candelabrum* "Blossoming Tree". Brass, silvered. Height 48 cm. 1913. Three clusters of coils curving downwards from the central column. Inv. No. 49/62

CITY ART GALLERY
IN THE LENBACH HOUSE

The City Art Gallery in the Lenbach House is the most recent among the larger collections of Munich. Its origins and its intentions are quite different from those of the older sister-museums, and the charm of the City Art Gallery lies to no small extent in the symbiosis between the private house belonging to Lenbach who dominated the artistic life of the late nineteenth century in Munich, and a museum which today is principally dedicated to the Munich avant-garde art of about 1910. In complete contrast to the direction given by Lenbach there has grown up within the gallery since 1957 a large number of works which are largely connected with artists of the *Blaue Reiter* group. The museum has devoted itself principally to painting; sculpture plays a minor part, and it is only very recently that important additions of sketches and prints have been added.

Although the purchase of the Lenbach property at the end of 1924 marked the opening of the museum, an art collection belonging to the city had already existed before this. The demand, the means and the works of art for such a collection had come from the townspeople. Since 1907 paintings and even money for a city gallery had been presented to the town from private sources on a number of occasions. After the First World War further donations were made and the need grew for a permanent home for the purchases which the city itself had made, mainly on charitable grounds. The temporary arrangements by which, for example, from 1911 fifty paintings were hung in the turret room of the Town Hall, without access for the public, or by which others were dispersed throughout various departments of administration, were just as unsatisfactory as directing them to the Historical Museum which was devoted to quite other interests. Finally it fell to the town, together with the state, to take over the task of fostering and encouraging contemporary art in Munich, just as the Wittelsbach court had done in previous times.

The year 1924 brought a favourable opportunity of solving all these problems, when Lenbach's widow offered to sell to the town on favourable terms the "Lenbach villa" in the Luisenstrasse. Moreover she offered to present to the town the collection made by the painter, who had died in 1904, on condition that in future it should be accessible to the public. The position of the property in the immediate neighbourhood of the Königsplatz, with its museums, and in no great distance from the two Pinakothek galleries, could not have been more favourable. The house built between 1883 and 1889 in "simple, elegant Renaissance" style is not only a tribute to its builder Lenbach, but it can even be called an architectural monument. The architect Gabriel von Seidl, who in the planning and execution of the work was no doubt influenced by Lenbach's ideas, has left his mark on the architecture of Munich at the turn of the century with the Bavarian National Museum and the German Museum. On 30th December 1924 the town council approved unanimously the agreements concluded "to the honour of Franz von Lenbach and to the continuing glory of Munich as cradle of the arts". We are indebted to the personal intervention of Küfner, the deputy mayor at that time, for this decision. Moreover further suggestions of his were also followed: the provision of funds to build a gallery near the Lenbach House, the establishment of a yearly budget for the purchase of works of art, and finally the appointment of an expert as director of the art collections. Happily the very man to make use of and develop these newly achieved opportunities for a city museum of art existed in the person of Eberhard Hanfstaengl, the first director of the house on the Luisenstrasse from 1924 to 1933.

A start was made immediately on the extension of the buildings, since the intention was to retain the Lenbach House with its gallery and the Lenbach collection as a complete unit. Between 1927 and 1929 the gallery itself was built to the plans of the City Engineer Hans Grässel as the north wing of the property; as a result of this in the north-west section which joins the old building to the gallery, there are some rooms on the top floor with lighting from above. The aim was to avoid spoiling the appearance of the Lenbach House but on the other hand by means of the gallery extensions to satisfy the demands of modern museum practice.

The solution worked out by Grässel and Hanfstaengl was a particularly happy one. The buildings arranged in a horse-shoe shape around a court which is open to the street appear in every way as an organic whole. The same is true of the interior. The skilfully chosen dimensions of the exhibition rooms, the variations between top lighting and window lighting, produce an effect not only pleasant in itself, but which more than anything else avoids possible discord between the rooms of the artist's house dating from the turn of the century and the newly erected exhibition buildings. The particular charm and merit of this museum lie precisely in the way in which it has taken into account the artistic tradition of Munich embodied in the Lenbach House and turned it to positive advantage.

The City Art Gallery had to justify its position alongside the larger state museums by expressing a character all of its own through its collections and exhibitions. The central idea was expressed in 1910 in a report which the city sought from the director of the state art galleries at that time, Hugo von Tschudi: that Munich painting of the nineteenth century "deserved to be fully represented in a public gallery". In the "Introduction" to the first catalogue of the City Art Gallery published in 1929 Hanfstaengl defines Munich art more closely and indicates how the museum based on it might be developed. "The gallery ... will only accept paintings by artists belonging to art circles in Munich ... the works brought together here must be the product of the Munich artistic environment and bear its characteristic mark. In the course of its artistic development Munich has proved its great power of assimilation ..., a power to which even the strongest individuality has had to yield. And the contents of the City Art Gallery are largely fashioned by this power." These statements meant that the choice of exhibits could not be limited to specific artists, groups or schools and excluded any local chauvinism in art. The introduction of Munich as the historical common factor had two important consequences for the museum, as Hanfstaengl pointed out: "The gallery has no limitations in time ... and its most important task is to serve living art."

The city owned more than a thousand paintings, but of these only twenty-five were suitable for the gallery. So Hanfstaengl was able to take over only "a very small proportion of the older paintings which are the property of the city" and for the rest was dependent on new purchases. The number of paintings grew uncommonly quickly, and by 1932 there were already 2,965 items listed. These included important names from the fifteenth to the twentieth centuries, from the late Gothic Munich painter Jan Polack to Hans Muelich, Horemans, Desmarées and Edlinger, the Court painters of the eighteenth century. Prominent among the many names from modern times are Kobell, Rottmann, Spitzweg, Haider, Leibl and Corinth. The Lenbach gallery too was enriched by the purchase of more than 100 paintings by the artist whose name it bears; as the museum of a single artist on this scale, together with Lenbach's house and studio, it is unique.

In 1933 Hanfstaengl went to Berlin as director of the State Collections of Paintings. But in the following years the policy of the gallery remained unchanged. A start was made in acquiring a series of sculptures by Adolf von Hildebrand, which was continued after the war.

In 1944 the south wing, which was Lenbach's studio, was destroyed except for the outer walls, and more than half of the central section and the additional gallery wing were lost. In September 1945 more than 100 paintings including 43 works by Lenbach and two by Leibl were stolen from their temporary storage in Lower Bavaria. The difficult task of making a new start fell to the director Arthur Rümann who was in charge of the City Art Collections from 1945 to 1956. By June 1947 the reconstruction of the gallery was sufficiently far advanced to start a series of post-war exhibitions with the "New Group". Between 1952 and 1954 the studio building was restored and three new rooms with top lighting were added. On the fiftieth anniversary of the death of Lenbach (1954) a catalogue was published. Rü- 58 mann resumed the tradition which had been interrupted by the war and the immediate pre-war period.

As well as frequent exhibitions, many notable acquisitions were made, such as five early paintings by Franz Marc, who up to this time had not been represented. In 1955 Rümann prepared another catalogue of the paintings. He was succeeded in 1956 by Hans Konrad Röthel. At the beginning of his period in office – and it was a considerable personal achievement – an event occurred of the greatest importance in the history of the gallery. On the occasion of her 80th birthday (19.2.1957) the artist Gabriele Münter presented to the City Art Gallery a large number of early works by Kandinsky: 88 paintings, 24 églomisé paintings, 116 water-colours and tempera paintings, 160 sketches, all his early engravings, as well as 28 sketchbooks and notebooks. Gabriele Münter also presented, from her own works, 25 paintings, her engravings, sketches, water-colours and églomisé paintings; in addition she made a gift of the paintings by her friends which were in her possession. Furthermore she assisted most generously in the acquisition of a large series of works of the period between 1900 and 1920. Names which had not appeared in the catalogues before 1957 were now represented by major works: some of the most important are Klee, Kandinsky, Jawlensky, Kubin, and Macke.

These gifts and acquisitions, by their number as well as by their importance, have essentially changed the nature of the gallery in the course of a few years. The original practice, from the early days of the gallery, of accepting only works which had some links with Munich had to be abandoned; indeed in the *Blauer Reiter*, on the evidence of Kubin, even nationality no longer played a part. The attention given since 1956 to the Munich avant-garde group of about 1910 turned the City Art Gallery, to a large extent, into an historical museum. It also resulted in a new policy formulated by Röthel: "In addition to the previous aims of the gallery, the museum now has the task of illustrating the rôle played by Munich in the development of modern painting as a whole." The most important acquisition of recent years, the Bernhard Koehler bequest, is entirely in line with this: in 1965 Frau Elly Koehler transferred to the city of Munich 23 works by Jawlensky, Macke, Marc and Niestlé. This presentation marks the recognition of the collection as the museum of the *Blaue Reiter* group.

The external appearance of the City Art Gallery has changed little since its reconstruction; it is still the Lenbach House. The addition of a further suite of rooms on the west side has presented greater possibilities for mounting exhibitions than ever before. Within the gallery the scene has been considerably altered by the wartime loss of former exhibits, by more modern museum techniques, and above all by the considerable increase in paintings of the "moderns". There are only a few rooms left in the centre section which still belong to the old Lenbach gallery with their walls lined in rich red, with joist ceilings and the furnishings of an earlier age.

DESCRIPTION OF ILLUSTRATIONS

159 Wilhelm Leibl. Born 1844 in Cologne, died in Würzburg 1900. *The Veterinary Surgeon Reindl in the Arbour.* Oil on cardboard, 26 × 19.5 cm. Signed: W. Leibl 90. Acquired 1927. Inv. No. G 307

160 Wilhelm von Kobell. Born 1766 in Mannheim, died in Munich 1853. *After the Hunt.* Oil on wood, 42 × 55.5 cm. Signed: Wilhelm v. Kobell 1833. Acquired 1933. Inv. No. 3098

161 Franz von Lenbach. Born 1836 in Schrobenhausen (Upper Bavaria), died in Munich 1904. *Portrait of Baron Schack* (study). Oil on canvas, 61 × 49 cm. About 1868/1870. Bequest of Lolo von Lenbach 1925. Inv. No. 28

162 Gabriele Münter. Born 1877 in Berlin, died in Murnau 1962. *Still Life in Grey.* Oil on cardboard, 34.3 × 50.5 cm. 1910. Signed: Münter. Bequest of Gabriele Münter 1957. Inv. No. GMS 662

163 Alexej von Jawlensky. Born 1867 in Kuslowo, died in Wiesbaden 1941. *Spanish Woman.* Oil on cardboard, 67 × 48.5 cm. 1913. Signed: A. Jawlensky/13. Acquired 1959. Inv. No. G 12556

164 August Macke. Born 1887 in Meschede, killed in action in Champagne 1914. *Promenade.* Oil on cardboard, 51 × 57 cm. 1913. Signed: August Macke 1913. Bequest of Bernhard Koehler 1965. Inv. No. G 13328

165 Franz Marc. Born 1880 in Munich, killed in action near Verdun 1916. *Blue Horse I.* Oil on canvas, 113 × 85 cm. 1911. Bequest of Bernhard Koehler 1965. Inv. No. G13324

166 a) Paul Klee. Born 1879 in Münchenbuchsee near Bern, died in Muralto-Locarno 1940. *Surprising Haul of Fish.* Pen-and-ink drawing, 17 × 5.8/7.4 cm. 1913. Signed: Klee 1913. 126. Bequest of Gabriele Münter 1957. Inv. No. GMS 13120

166 b) Klee. *Suburb* (North Munich). Mixed technique, 12.1×19.4 cm. 1913. Signed: Klee 1913. 199. Presented by Gabriele Münter 1962. Inv. No. G 13120

167 Wassily Kandinsky. Born 1866 in Moscow, died in Neuilly-sur-Seine 1944. *Woman in Moscow*. Oil on canvas, 108.8×108.8 cm. About 1912. Signed (on back): Kandinsky Woman in Moscow. Bequest of Gabriele Münter 1957. Inv. No. GMS 73

168 Kandinsky. *Improvisation – Deluge*. Oil on canvas, 95× 150 cm. 1913. Signed (on back): Kandinsky 1913/Deluge/ Improvisation. Bequest of Gabriele Münter 1957. Inv. No. GMS 76

The Glyptothek on the Königsplatz

BAVARIAN STATE COLLECTIONS
OF PAINTINGS

1500

Albertus Durerus Noricus
ipsum me proprijs sic effin-
gebam coloribus ætatis
anno XXVIII.

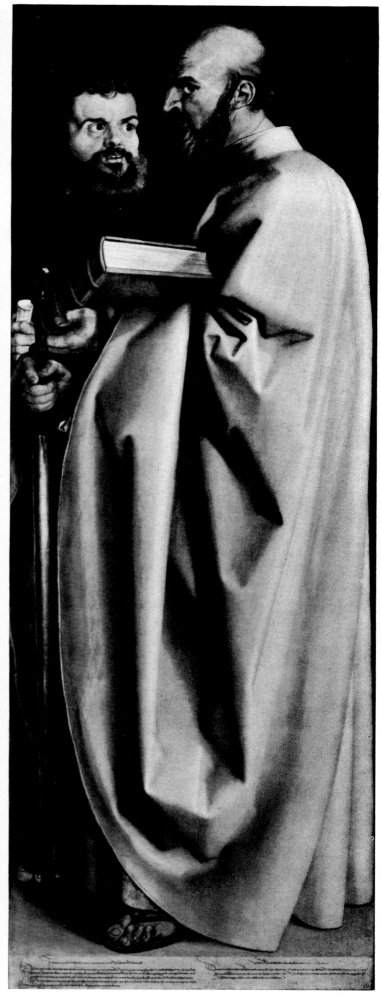

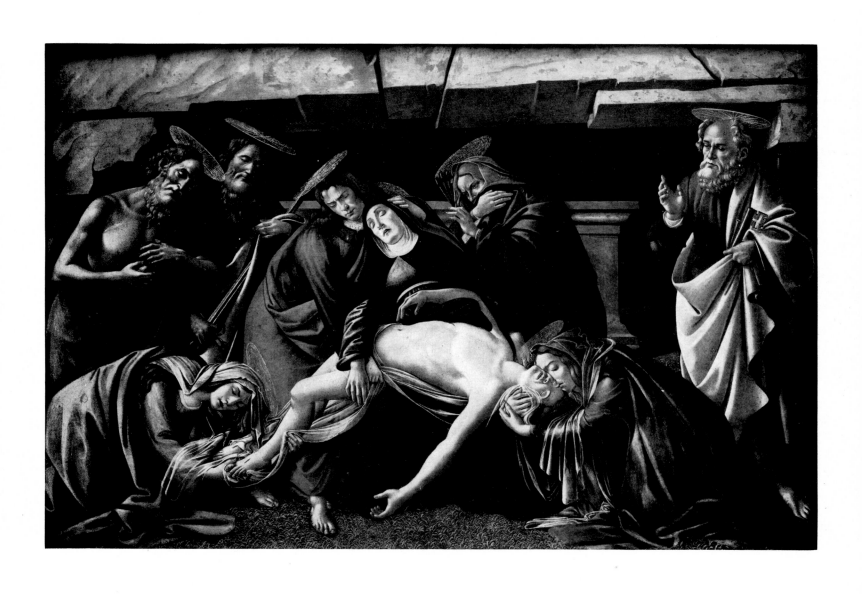

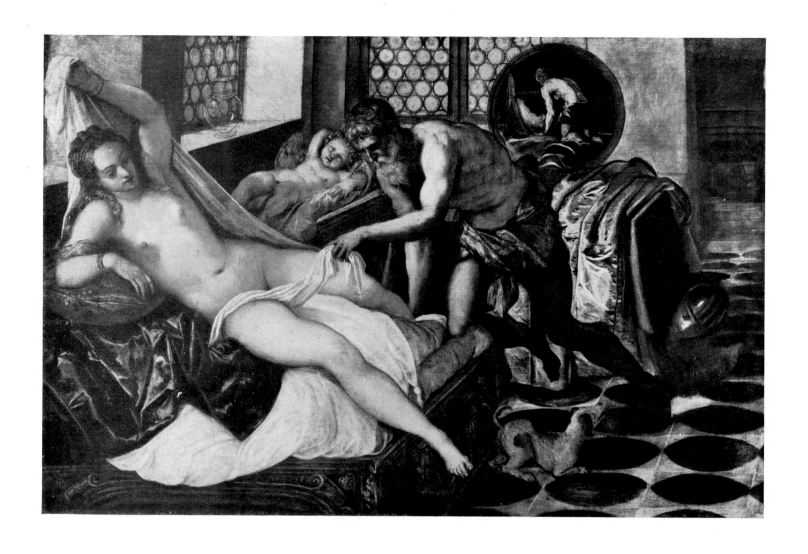

18

23

33

38

40

45

47

48

53

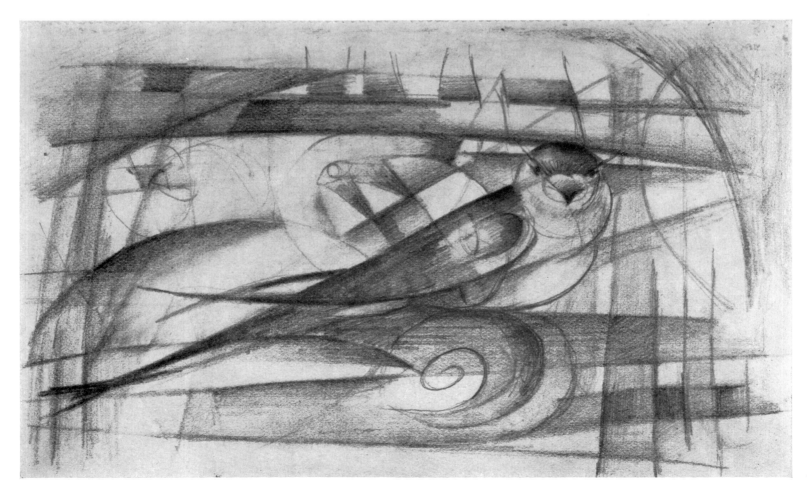

BAVARIAN NATIONAL MUSEUM

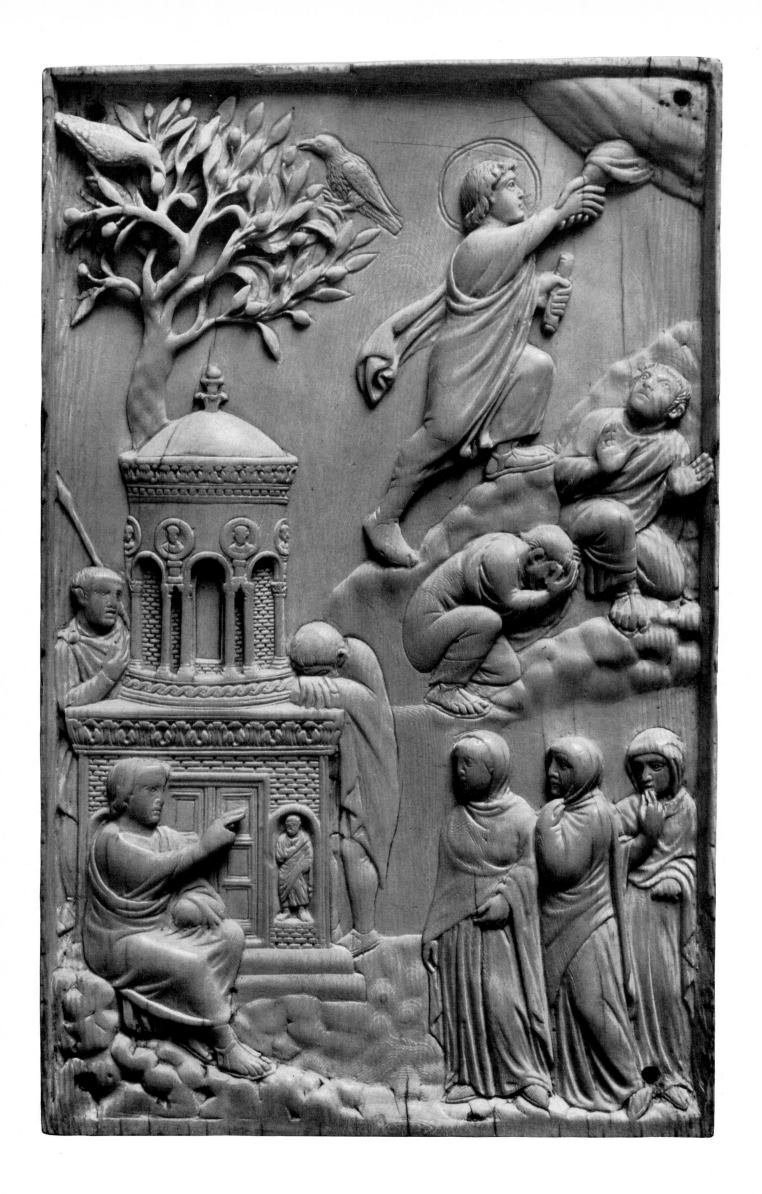

60

64

66

68

69

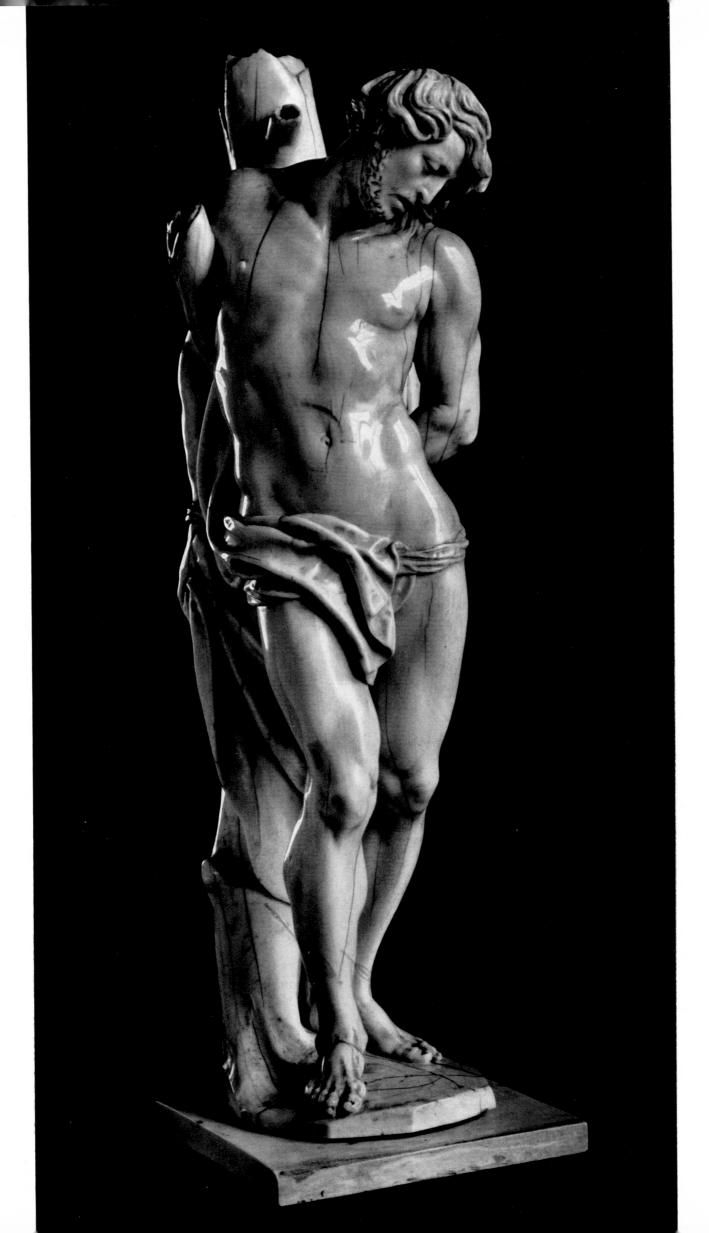

COLLECTIONS OF CLASSICAL ART AND GLYPTOTHEK

85 Marble Statue of a Youth ("The Apollo of Tenea"). Greek work of the 6th century B.C.

86 Head of a Dying Warrior, one of the figures from the east pediment of the Temple of Aphaia at Aegina. Greek, about 490 B.C.

87 a) Head of Homer. Roman copy in marble of a Greek original in bronze of about 450 B.C.

87 b) Head of the Medusa. Roman copy in marble of a Greek original of the 5th century B.C.

88 Tomb Relief of Mnesarete. Attic work of about 380 B.C.

89 a) Head of Aphrodite. The head is a copy from the "Capitoline Venus" of the beginning of the 3rd century B.C.

89 b) Head of a Sleeping Satyr (the "Barberini Faun"). Greek work of about 220 B.C.

90 a) Bronze Statuette of Poseidon. 2nd century B.C.

90 b) Golden Diadem. Macedonian-Greek work of the 4th/3rd centuries B.C.

91 Marble Bust of Augustus wearing the civic crown. Roman work of the second quarter of the 1st century A.D.

92 a) Attic Amphora, an example of geometric vase painting. Early 8th century B.C.

92 b) Jug from Rhodes with Animal Friezes. About 630 B.C.

93 a) Attic Mixing Vessel. About 480 B.C.

93 b) Attic Amphora by the Andocides Painter. About 520 B.C.

94 Attic Drinking Bowl by Execias. About 530 B.C.

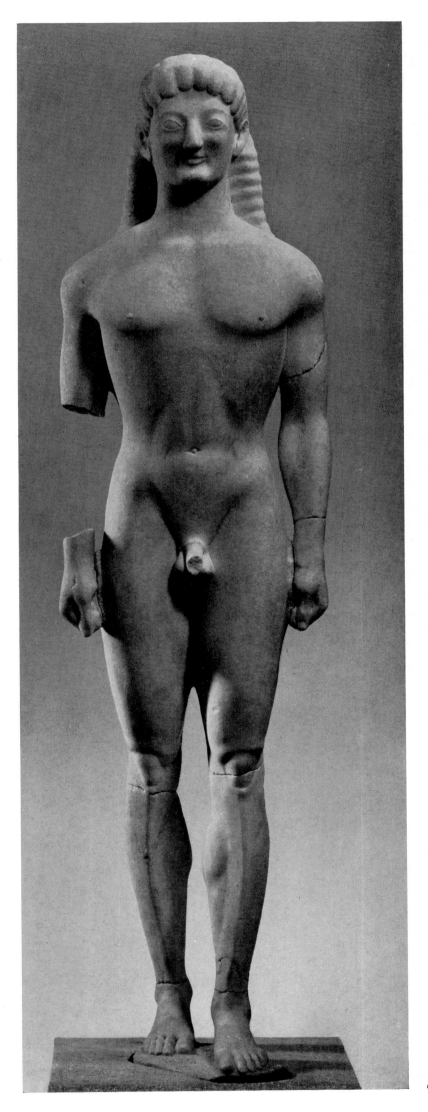

93

EGYPTIAN COLLECTION

RESIDENCE MUSEUM AND TREASURY

OTHO.M.COM.PALAT.WITELSPACHEN.BOIARIÆ.DVX

GERMANICI IMPERII MAIESTATEM ADVERSV
GRÆCORVM ARTES ET FACTIOSOS ALIOS V
MINISQVE REPVLSOS ASSERIT AN.MCLII

123

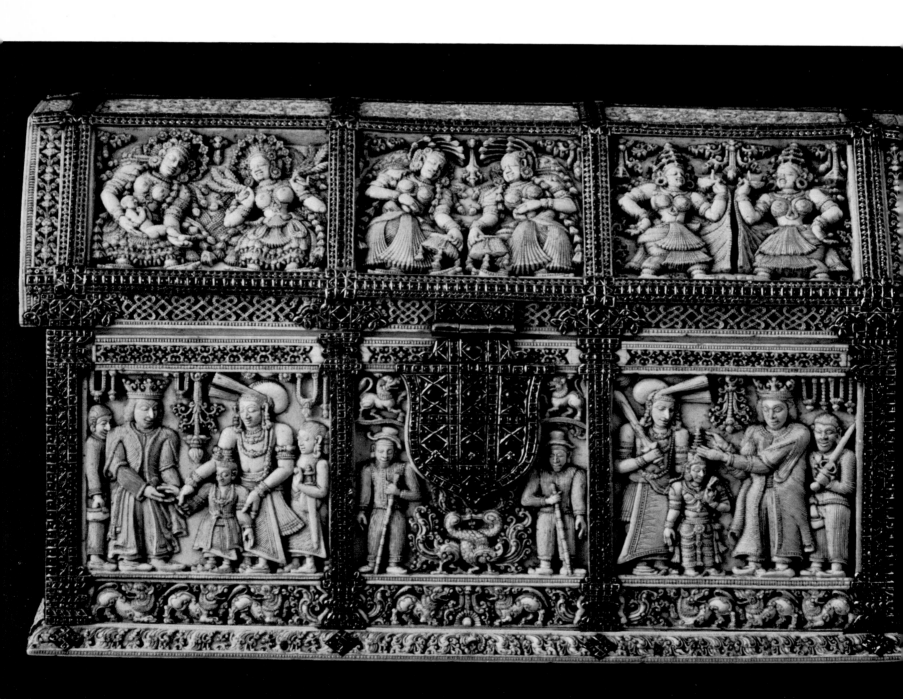

MUSEUM OF ETHNOLOGY

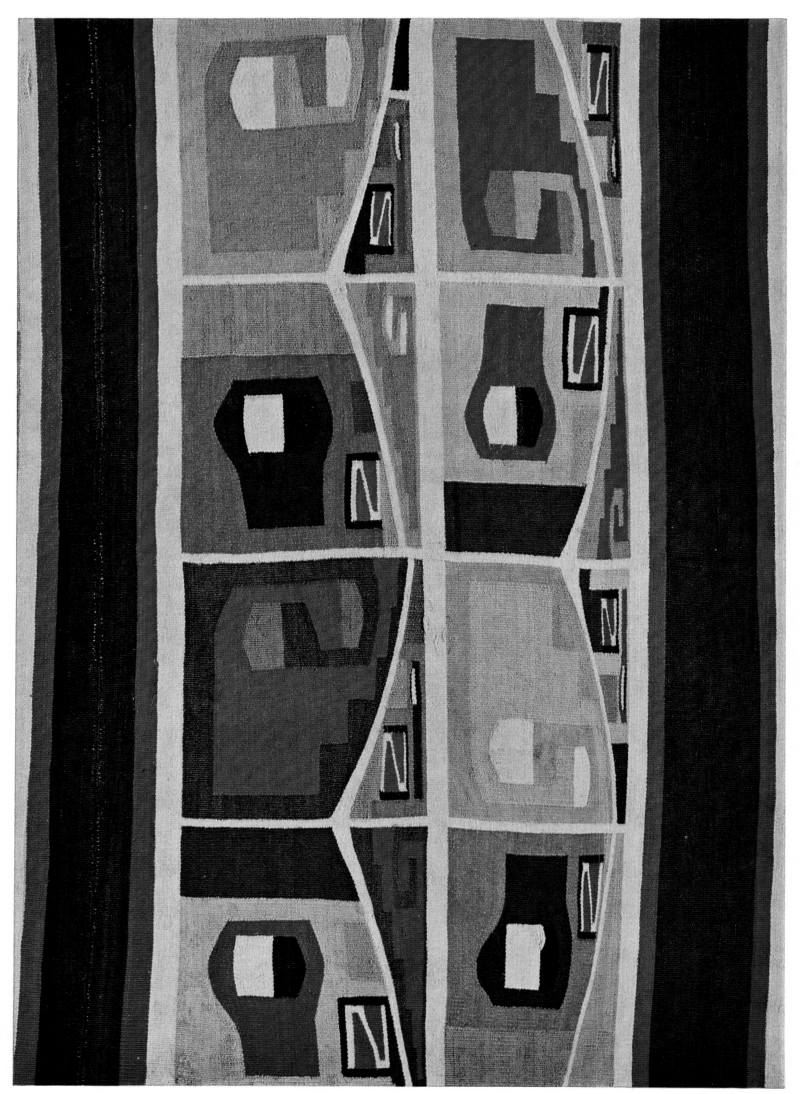

Classical Coins and Engraved Gems

143   1. Athens, Attica. Tetradrachma, about 510 B.C.

       2. Syracuse, Sicily. Tetradrachma, about 410 B.C.

       3. Scarabaeus, rock-crystal, late 6th century B.C.

       4. Cask-shaped Gem, agate, 5th century B.C.

144   1. Miletus, Ionia. Stater, about 600 B.C.

       2. Ephesus, Ionia. Stater, 6th century B.C.

       3. Acragas, Sicily. Decadrachma, about 410 B.C.

       4. Rome, Septimius Severus. Aureus, A.D. 202

       5. Ticinum (Pavia), Constantine I. Medal of about A.D. 315

       6. Sardis, Achaios. Stater, 220–213 B.C.

       7. Rome, Hadrian. Sestertius, A.D. 125–128

       8. India, Mahmud III. Presentation Coin of five tankas, A.D. 1463/64

European Coins of 9th–16th Centuries

145   1. Emperor Ludwig the Pious, 814–840. Gold Solidus without date of minting

       2. Germany, King Philipp or Otto IV. One-sided Silver Pfennig, about 1210

       3. Falkenstein in the Harz, Count Burkhard II. One-sided Silver Pfennig, about 1170–1180

       4. Bavaria, Duke Albrecht V, 1550–1579. Ducat without date stamp

       5. Augsburg, Quadruple Taler of 1625

       6. Archbishopric of Salzburg, Medal, 1593, with value of 6 talers

       7. Aragon, King Ferdinand II the Catholic, 1479–1516. Ten-ducat piece without date stamp

       8. Dauphiny, France, King François I. Quadruple Teston of 1537

       9. Milan, Emperor Karl V (Duke of Milan 1535–1556). Ducatone, no date of minting

146   1. Germany, King Philipp or Otto IV. One-sided Silver Pfennig of about 1210

       2. Falkenstein in the Harz, Count Burkhard II. One-sided Silver Pfennig of about 1170–1180

       3. Italy, Cameo, 13th century

European Medals

146   4. Gilded Bronze Medal in the honour of Anne of Brittany. Unknown artist, 1494

147   1. Model for a Medal by Friedrich Hagenauer. Augsburg, about 1535

       2. Model for a Medal by Matthes Gebel. Nuremberg, dated 1529

       3. Model for a Medal by Christoph Weiditz. Augsburg, dated 1530

       4. Golden Jewel in an enamelled setting worked in gold, probably by Paul Zeggin. Munich, 1623/24

       5. Bronze Medal by Hans Schwarz. South Germany, dated 1520

       6. Bronze Medal, probably by Hubert Gerhard. Munich, dated 1585

148   1. Lead Medal by Valentin Maler. Nuremberg, about 1585

       2. Bronze Medal by Antonio Pisano. Made about 1445

       3. Silver Medal by Jacopo da Trezzo. Made in 1555

1

2

3

4

1

2

3

4

5

6

7

8

144

1

2

3

4

1

2

3

CITY ART GALLERY
IN THE LENBACH HOUSE

159

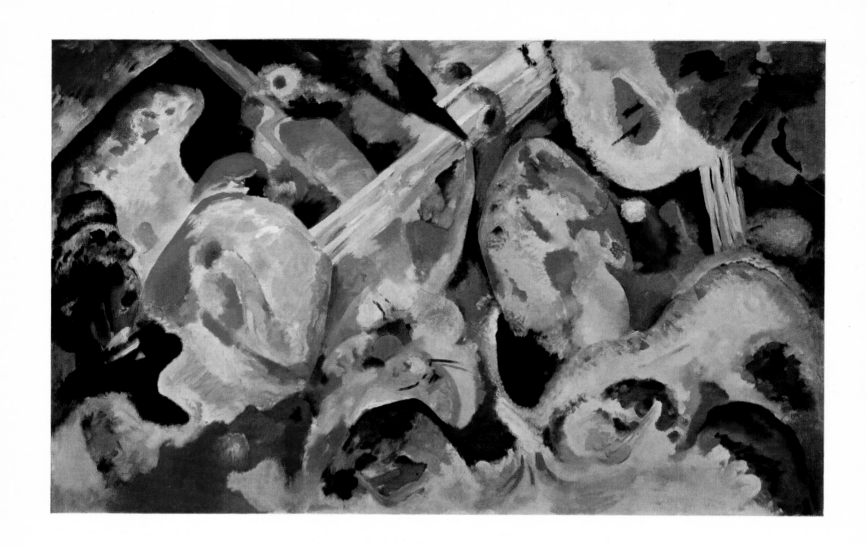